PRAISE FOR *AN IMPOSSIBLE WIFE*

"Siddoway tackles the impact of mental illness on marriage in her moving memoir, a follow-up to An Impossible Life. Despite such a painful topic, Siddoway effectively draws readers in with rare fluency and power, highlighting both the unequivocal love between her parents and their exhaustive crusade to take back their lives. This gut-wrenching examination of one family's tenacity in the face of debilitating mental illness is a lighthouse of hope."

— BOOK LIFE, PUBLISHER WEEKLY

"The brave and vital work of this family to share their individual and shared stories so openly and without reservation is a gift to all readers. An Impossible Wife is a moving story of love, heartbreak, and the impacts of mental illness on every member of the family."

— INDIE READER

"An emotional account of how Mitch and Sonja's marriage remained a true love story—one in which they encountered and overcame extraordinary challenges. Throughout the work, Siddoway's writing is journalistically precise and confessionally candid in its revelations. As a result, this book is not only an impressively nuanced depiction of mental illness, but also a moving account of an inextinguishable love. An affecting work about maintaining devotion amid life's difficulties."

— KIRKUS REVIEW

An Impossible Wife

AN IMPOSSIBLE WIFE

Why He Stayed: A True Story of Love, Marriage, and Mental Illness

by
Rachael Siddoway

©2021 The Gap Press

All rights reserved. This book or any portion thereof may not be reproduced or used in any manner whatsoever without the express written permission of the publisher except for the use of brief quotations in a book review.

Published by The Gap Press, LLC

An Impossible Wife / Rachael Siddoway – 1st edition

Edited by Joel Pierson

Cover Photo by Rachael Siddoway

ISBN: 978-1-7336194-4-8 (KDP paperback)
ISBN: 978-1-7336194-3-1 (Kindle)

CONTENTS

Author's Note ix
The Invitation xi

Chapter 1   Rock Bottom   1
Chapter 2   The Nemelkas   5
Chapter 3   A First Date   11
Chapter 4   The Interrogation   15
Chapter 5   The Eight-Date Wait   19
Chapter 6   Full Disclosure   23
Chapter 7   The Train   29
Chapter 8   Josephine   35
Chapter 9   Sonja Slipping Away   39
Chapter 10   A Religious Divide   43
Chapter 11   The Wild Ride   47
Chapter 12   Risking It All   51
Chapter 13   OCD   57
Chapter 14   Bathing   65
Chapter 15   The Feelings Box   69
Chapter 16   Dinner Party   73
Chapter 17   Secrets in Plain Sight   77
Chapter 18   David   81
Chapter 19   The Fight Pattern   85
Chapter 20   A New Normal   89
Chapter 21   Reinforcements   95
Chapter 22   The Emergency Room   103
Chapter 23   Drugged   107
Chapter 24   Visiting Hours   111

Chapter 25	The Diagnosis	115
Chapter 26	Coming Home	121
Chapter 27	Doctoral Program	123
Chapter 28	The Job Search	129
Chapter 29	Unexpected News	133
Chapter 30	The Phone Call	137
Chapter 31	Ebay	141
Chapter 32	Lock Me Up	145
Chapter 33	Therapy	147
Chapter 34	A Helping Hand	151
Chapter 35	Lincoln Has Enough	153
Chapter 36	Snapped	155
Chapter 37	The Next Morning	157
Chapter 38	The Bedside Talk	161
Chapter 39	Awake	163
Chapter 40	The Holidays	167
Chapter 41	Losing Lincoln	171
Chapter 42	Appearances	173
Chapter 43	The Unexpected	175
Chapter 44	Heartache	177
Chapter 45	Relationships	181
Chapter 46	Fighting for Love	183
Chapter 47	Freedom to Choose	187
Epilogue		191
Chapter 1	Dear Santa	197

AUTHOR'S NOTE

An Impossible Wife has been a labor of love. The hardest book I have written to date. My father is an extremely private person, and getting him to share his deepest feelings was no easy task. While interviewing my dad about his marriage and my mother's mental illness, many silent tears were shared. I want to thank my dad for bravely opening up and making himself vulnerable. He agreed to this book, not only to support my mother's mental health advocacy work, but to help other people who have loved ones struggling with mental illness.

While there is information shared about me and my brothers, this book does not go into detail about how we felt or our lives. Our family understands this will leave you with questions. My parents feel strongly that my brothers and I should have the right to speak for ourselves. This book, *An Impossible Wife*, is my father's truth.

THE INVITATION

It doesn't interest me to know where you live or how much money you have. I want to know if you can get up after the night of grief and despair, weary and bruised to the bone and do what needs to be done to feed the children.

It doesn't interest me who you know or how you came to be here. I want to know if you will stand in the centre of the fire with me and not shrink back.

—Oriah Mountain Dreamer[1]

---

1 By Oriah "Mountain Dreamer" House from her book *The Invitation* © 1999. Published by HarperONE, San Francisco. All rights reserved. Presented with permission of the author. www.oriah.org

CHAPTER 1

Rock Bottom

Columbia, Missouri
December 13, 2015

Ambulance lights flashed through the windows of our house as my dad held my mom in his arms. Bright reds and blues swirled against the brick house, waking up our usually quiet street.

She's barely breathing. He panicked as he frantically checked the labels of the empty pill bottles. Lamictal, Geodon, Ativan.

What was she thinking? Her head lay heavy in his lap before the paramedics took her.

"She took these." My dad's shaky hands showed the medic the pill bottles.

"You the husband?" The medic glanced at the labels.

"Yes." He nodded.

"Come with us."

Neighbors stood on their lawns, watching paramedics rush my mom's unconscious body out of the house on a stretcher. My dad stepped inside the ambulance and watched his wife remain unresponsive as two large IVs slipped through the veins in her hands.

The sirens sounded as they sped down the streets, not stopping for red lights. The IV bags swayed with each bump in the road. Swallowed up in the chaos, my dad sought out his faith for a moment of stillness. He pleaded with God to save my mother's life.

As they entered the hospital, he could hear the whispers from the staff: "It's the CEO and his wife." But none of their comments was registering. In that moment, he was stuck on the thoughts, *Will my wife live? What did my son see?*

My sixteen-year-old brother, Lincoln, and my mom had been fighting right before she had stormed off, locked herself in the bathroom, and swallowed hundreds of pills. Their fights had become habitual, but none had ever escalated to something like this before.

My parents' friends Dean and Lorie had their son take Lincoln to their house, but my dad couldn't pinpoint when.

Once inside the ER, a team of nurses and doctors quickly surrounded my mom's body on the stretcher. Nurses cut off my mom's clothes as doctors promptly began pumping her stomach, trying to force out the pills she had swallowed. They pushed charcoal down her throat, hoping it would absorb the rest. The medical team worked aggressively to save her, and all my dad could do was stand by and watch as they hooked up EKG leads to her chest and ran an intubation tube down her throat to keep her breathing. He had continually been the one she depended on to keep her alive, but in this moment, he had no influence on her ability to live or die. She lay motionless as every tube, needle, and lead went into her body. My dad stood like a man on a distant shore, forced to watch his beloved ship slowly go under.

"We'll have to wait and see how her body responds to the overdose." The doctor's voice broke through his thoughts.

My dad reluctantly shifted his gaze from his wife to the doctor.

"We'll put her in the ICU and do all we can to save her, but it's hard to say right now what the outcome will be," the doctor apprehensively admitted.

Even though she had talked about wanting to kill herself hundreds of times over their twenty-three-year marriage, he was utterly unprepared for the day she might die. He touched the scratchy hospital blanket laid across her legs, hoping to feel some sense of reality, but no matter what he touched, saw, or smelled, the present moment remained distant to him.

My dad had decades of experience on how to remain levelheaded during my mom's episodes. He'd administer her medicine, brush her hair, and cuddle her while they watched a movie until she fell asleep. If that didn't work, my parents made trips to the ER for an IV of Ativan, and suicidal ideations could lead to an admission to the psych ward. He knew how all those situations ended. But my dad had never dealt with this—an actual suicide attempt.

This was a level of the illness he had never seen, and my dad didn't know what came next. As he sat in my mom's hospital room, unable to hold her without the fear of moving her breathing tube, he felt sharp cracks spreading across his heart, as thin and precise as pencil lines, and he knew for the first time his heart was actually breaking.

"Dad?" Lincoln stood timidly in the doorway.

"I'm sorry, Lincoln," my dad carefully said.

Lincoln said nothing, but each time he glanced at our mom, unconscious and hooked up to multiple tubes, he would quickly look away. He refused to get too close to her. Lincoln must have been grappling with the fact that she had attempted suicide during a fight they'd had.

"Is Mom going to live?" Lincoln asked.

As much as my dad wanted to shelter him from the truth, he knew he needed to be honest. "I don't know," he answered quietly.

Lincoln started to cry, and my dad grabbed him, wrapping his arms tightly around him.

How did I get here? he wondered.

<hr />

My parents' love story is not the kind I grew up watching in Disney movies. Their love is a complicated love, and at times an impossible one. Yet I think their story is worth sharing, despite its absence of simplicity. It's through great struggle that heroes are realized, and it's through even greater sorrow that two young people can age into one. And that's exactly what happened to my parents. This is their love story.

CHAPTER 2

The Nemelkas

Mapleton, Utah
Spring 1991

Mitch Wasden stood at the Nemelkas' large and intimidating front door, holding the strings to a dozen colorful balloons. For being in a small town, the Nemelkas' house was opulent and by far the largest in the community. Mitch's younger brother Jon was asking Allyson Nemelka to a high school dance. Mitch was both his chauffeur and delivery boy, given that Jon lacked the driver's license and the courage to deliver the balloons himself. Jon waited in the car, and Mitch rang the doorbell. The long melody echoed inside the house, and soon after, the door opened.

"Hi!" A beautiful girl with long black hair and stunning green eyes stood before him. He stared at her, trying to remember why he had come.

"Um ... I'm Mitch, Jon's brother." He suddenly felt awkward and pivoted on his right foot. "He's asking Allyson to a school dance, and I'm his delivery boy." He gestured to the balloons.

"Oh, that's so fun!" She laughed. "She's not here right now, but I'll give them to her." She took the balloons excitedly. "So, are you in school?" She fearlessly looked right into his stone-blue eyes.

"I'm a sophomore at Utah Valley Community College, but I want to transfer to BYU," he answered, unable to look away.

"Oh my gosh, I'm a sophomore at BYU!"

"Would you recommend it?"

"Well, to be honest," she said as she leaned against the doorframe, "I was forced to go there. I really wanted to go to Utah State. So, can I really recommend a place I never wanted to be at?"

"Good point." He shrugged.

"But I can recommend a class. Do you like poetry?" She casually pointed at him.

"Actually, I do. Who's your favorite poet?" he asked.

"Easy. Dylan Thomas."

"Do not go gentle into that good night, Old age should burn and rave at close of day," Mitch recited in his best Dylan Thomas voice.

"Rage, rage against the dying of the light," she chimed in.

"So, we both love a poem about death?" Mitch laughed.

"Well, that's not all it's about. I think he's reminding us life is short, so we should not only embrace it, but fight for it."

"Right! It's like a call to carpe diem as his dad is dying." Mitch paused. "So, who exactly are you?"

"Oh, sorry! I'm Sonja, Allyson's older sister."

Mitch's family had recently moved to Mapleton, Utah, from Lubbock, Texas, but he still knew of the Nemelkas. Everyone in Mapleton knew the Nemelka family. They were one of the most affluent and accomplished families in town. They were patrons of the local art museum, where a section of the museum was named after Sonja's mom: the Ingrid F. Nemelka Christmas Lamb Gallery.

Her dad was rumored to have worked with some very colorful and questionable business associates. A story he proudly told around town was of a business partner who took a chainsaw to his own desk, cutting it clean in half and threatening to take everyone down with him if the deal went under. Mitch had heard many stories about the Nemelkas but had never heard of Sonja.

"Would you like to come in?" she asked. Mitch looked back at the car and saw Jon leaned back in the passenger seat.

"Sure," he said, stepping inside.

The house was more than just large. Many of the windows were of stained-glass flowers or birds, and the wall moldings were carved with gold-leaf hearts and wreaths.

"I'll give you a tour." Sonja laughed, finding his wide-eyed reaction amusing.

She trotted up one side of the expansive staircase, her black hair swinging behind her. Mitch took one step before noticing the large gold chandelier above them. The vaulted ceiling itself was a work of art; the chandelier hung in the center of a sky-blue mural in which horses were sculpted right out of the ceiling, encircling the chandelier fixture. Each horse was painted to look realistic while also accented in gold leaf.

"Are you coming?" She stood at the top of the staircase, looking back at his head tilted up at the ceiling.

"Yeah, I'm coming." He ran up the stairs.

She opened a door with a realistic etching of a horse in the glass. "This is my dad's office."

Mitch looked around the dark-wood office, at the bronze statues of horses and eagles on shelves and tables. "Your dad must like horses."

"He loves them. He races, mostly Appaloosas." Sonja pointed up a narrow stairway, where racing trophies sat on the second story of the office.

She continued the tour through several bedrooms, living spaces, an indoor swimming pool, and an enormous game room. Sonja stopped to sit inside a telephone booth inside the house.

"And that's our racquetball court," she said, pointing at an opposing glass wall.

"As one has," Mitch said with a casual, dry wit.

"You're funny." She smiled. "Come on." She tugged him. "I want to show you something really cool." She walked into a closet, motioning for him to follow. "I don't normally show people this room, so consider yourself lucky."

"Interesting ...," he said as he looked around at the coat hangers. "No offense, but this is one of the more underwhelming rooms of the house."

"Just wait." She slid her fingers around the wood-paneled walls, looking for something.

"Please don't tell me you have secret rooms too," he said sarcastically.

"Ah, here it is." She grabbed a wire hanger and touched it to a metal bolt holding a coat hook to the wall. *Guzzzzzzzz.* A soft vibration buzzed through the wall—and then a single click. Sonja pushed the wall open. Mitch's jaw might as well have fallen to the floor.

"You're kidding." He ducked his head under the hangers clinking on the rack and stepped inside the secret room. Stacks of paintings were leaned against the walls, and a giant safe sat at the back of the room.

"What is all this?" Mitch looked around.

"My dad's art collection. He loves to rotate the paintings on our walls."

"So, what's in the safe? Must be pretty important if it's in a secret room."

"I don't know exactly, but my grandpa has some silver bars in there."

"Silver bars?" Mitch said, raising his eyebrows.

"My grandpa turned his money into silver and then buried it in his backyard. He doesn't trust banks. But when my dad got a safe, he dug them up and brought them here."

"I think I need to meet your grandpa."

"Okay, last room. And then maybe I'll let you go." She winked.

Sonja took him into an all-white room with white furniture. A large oil painting of her parents hung over a marble fireplace, and oil paintings of the seven children, some with their spouses, lined the surrounding walls. One by one, she introduced him to each portrait, and it was clear to Mitch she deeply loved her family.

Her energy was contagious, and he found himself drawn to her. She seemed happy to be with him, even though they had just met. Sonja was full of light and laughed easily, whereas Mitch was calm with moments of clever wit. She asked him a million questions.

Did his family like Mapleton? What were his plans for the summer? How did he like college? And Mitch happily answered each one. The two of them lost track of time, talking like lifelong friends whose paths had finally crossed again.

"If you transfer to BYU, you have to let me know," she said, casually dropping her hand on his arm.

Mitch's heart stopped.

He looked down at her hand lightly resting on his arm and chose to say nothing. Mitch really wanted to ask her out, yet he felt unsure. Sonja's dad was very proud of his children's accomplishments and often shared those accomplishments with people. Mitch had heard that Sonja's older sister had married the son of a prominent political family from Arizona who was number one at his law school. A brother had married Miss Georgia Teen, while another brother was going to Wharton's MBA program, which was ranked number one in the United States. This set a high bar.

Sonja walked Mitch to the front door. "So, should I be expecting more deliveries from you?"

"That all depends on how well the dance goes." Mitch smiled.

"Well, then I hope it goes well." Sonja crossed her fingers.

He walked the stone steps back to his car with his heart and logic conflicted. In high school, Mitch was a straight-C student. As a natural-born pragmatist, he only pulled up his grades his senior year because that was the year colleges would care about most. With no prestigious bloodline or high-powered career in the works, he reasoned he and Sonja wouldn't be a fit. By the time he got in his car, he had talked himself out of ever asking her on a date.

"Where have you been? I have been waiting in the car for like two hours!" Jon was furious.

"I just met Allyson's sister; she's really cool." Mitch started up the car.

"Jeez, by how long you were in there, you better have at least asked her out." Jon leaned back.

"Sorry to disappoint you, but I don't think I'm her type. Plus, she's going to Switzerland for the summer."

Just put her out of your mind, he told himself as he drove away. Despite this being their first meeting, it was harder to do than expected. Sonja was a girl one didn't easily forget.

CHAPTER 3

A First Date

Provo, Utah
Fall 1991

Summer came and went, and to Mitch's own surprise, he successfully transferred to Brigham Young University. It had been six months since he had met Sonja, and over that time, he had heard through a mutual friend that she had a boyfriend serving a two-year church mission in England.

A fall breeze blew throughout the campus as Mitch walked to his history class. He tucked his hands in his pockets, enjoying the change in season. Sonja's older brother Joe passed him on his way to class. They knew each other from being in the same student church congregation. They gave each other a nod, and Mitch kept walking. After class, he stopped to get lunch, and Joe passed him a second time.

"Hello again." Joe laughed. BYU was a huge campus, with around twenty-five thousand students, so later that day, when Mitch passed Joe for the third time, he decided to stop and talk to him.

"How was your summer?" Mitch asked.

"Good, good. You know, I was thinking you should ask out my sister Sonja," Joe suddenly said.

His suggestion caught Mitch off guard. He wanted to admit

that he had thought about asking Sonja on a date for the last six months but instead gave one of the many reasons why he hadn't. "I thought she had a boyfriend serving a mission."

"Yeah. But it's nothing serious." Joe waved his hand in the air.

"I don't know. Seems like an unchristian thing to do to a missionary," Mitch joked. He wanted to take Sonja out, but the thought of actually doing it made him nervous.

"Listen, you really should take her out. Let me give you her number." Joe wrote down her number on a piece of paper and handed it to Mitch.

Mitch went to the cafeteria and pulled that paper out of his backpack. He had essentially been given the Nemelka family blessing to ask Sonja on a date. Maybe it was fate that he had kept running into her brother, or perhaps it wasn't, but either way, he hurriedly punched her number in the school phone before he lost his nerve. The phone rang over and over, but no one answered. He tried calling her for two weeks, but her phone continued to ring with no answer.

While driving home from school, he passed a gas station with a payphone and thought he should try calling her just one last time. Mitch pulled over and dropped a quarter into the coin slot; it rang once before her roommate picked up.

"Hey, is Sonja there?" he asked.

"Yeah, one sec." She covered the phone and was whispering something to someone as Mitch waited.

"This is Sonja." Her friendly voice came through the phone.

"It's Mitch," he said right as a semitruck honked down the road.

"Where are you?"

"I'm at a gas station," he answered.

"Oh, do you need a ride?" she asked, concerned.

"No, no. I've been trying to call you for three days." He made sure to decrease the number of days he'd been trying to reach her, as fourteen days could appear overeager. "I just pulled over at a gas station payphone and thought I'd try one last time."

"Our phone has been broken, but it just got fixed."

He gathered his courage. "I was wondering if you might want to go out with me next weekend. I was thinking maybe Saturday."

"Yes! I'd love to." She sounded surprised.

"Great, I'll pick you up Saturday at six."

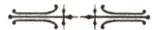

※

As a poor college student, Mitch had planned a creative but inexpensive date. Normally he didn't lack confidence on dates, but on this occasion, he had doubts about what he'd planned for the evening. He wondered if Sonja would find the date odd or quirky. He sat in his car outside her apartment and accepted that there was no turning back now. He'd just have to be himself and let the evening play out as it was meant to. Mitch stood on her doorstep at six o'clock on the dot.

Sonja opened the door, and he looked at her in amazement. She was even prettier than he remembered. She wore a white cotton blouse she'd bought that summer in Switzerland with blue jeans and black velvet shoes. He thought to himself that she looked both casual and elegant. Her black hair had grown out even longer over the summer and was now down to her waist. *At least we both wore jeans*, Mitch thought. He had opted for a red flannel shirt and hiking boots. He was hitting casual but had missed elegant or refined by a wide margin.

"You ready?" he asked.

"Yep!" She grabbed a jacket. "What are you holding?" She suspiciously peered around his back.

Mitch excitedly revealed two balsa wood airplanes, the kind you buy in a toy store for $1.50 and assemble yourself.

"I'm holding in my hands the best date you've ever had." He proudly smiled. "Have you ever flown one of these?" he asked, handing her an airplane.

"I can't say that I have." She held the plane.

"Good. Then that means I'm going to win," he replied smugly.

"We'll see." She rolled her eyes.

They sat in the grass assembling their planes, and Mitch was glad to see not too many people were on campus that night.

"So, the plan is we're having an air show. And believe it or not, these planes are going to provide us hours of fun and competitive banter," he said, slipping the two wood pieces together.

"Oh, really, competitive banter?" She laughed. "Well, I've recently been on an airplane, so I might have the edge." She winked confidently.

They pitched their planes off the top stories of buildings and through fountains. They competed for distance, aerial aerobatics, and speed. Within a few hours, a simple date became Mitch's favorite date, and it was all because of her. They plopped down onto the ledge of a large fountain, sitting knee to knee. He placed his hand causally over hers, and it made his heart skip.

"My dream is to be able to fit everything I own in my car so I can go anywhere I want," he said.

"Ahh, complete freedom! Sign me up!" She sighed. "So, tell me, what career do you see for yourself in the future?"

"That's easy. I want to be a history professor." He laced his fingers with hers.

"I think you'd be good at that." She put her head on his shoulder.

With her, he felt like he was talking to a best friend. She was easy to be with, and he felt safe sharing his world view with her. At the end of the evening, Mitch walked her back to her apartment.

"Thanks for the date. I had a lot of fun with you," she said.

"Yeah, I get that a lot. All the girls like me. I'm kind of a catch." He shrugged, and she burst out laughing.

"I had a great time with you too." He leaned in to kiss her cheek.

He didn't know how he knew, but somewhere in his soul, Mitch knew he had found his person.

CHAPTER 4

The Interrogation

After they had been dating for several weeks, Sonja invited Mitch over to meet some of her family. He sat in a large, deep chair next to a fireplace with stone hearts chiseled throughout it. Sonja's family gathered in the living room, surrounding him. He had no idea an interrogation was about to begin, with himself as the person of interest.

"Where did you grow up?" Sonja's dad asked.

"Solvang, California."

"And what's your father's profession?" Her father leaned back in his chair.

"He was a dentist, but he's retired now," Mitch answered.

"Wow. How old was he when he retired?" her dad asked, rubbing his hands together.

"I think fifty-two."

"How does a dentist retire so young? He must've had money somewhere else."

"My parents made some money selling land in California, and we lived on a tight budget."

"How do you like Utah?" Sonja's mom asked.

"I like it. Growing up, I spent every summer in Scipio, Utah, working on my grandparents' farm, so I'm somewhat acquainted."

"What type of farm was it?" David folded a newspaper over his knee.

"We raised cattle. My brothers and I would begin each summer by branding the cattle, mending fences, and moving sprinkler pipes on the two-thousand-acre farm. The most crucial task was raising three alfalfa crops for the cattle to feed on in the winter," Mitch answered, looking around at Sonja's other siblings, who were mostly staying quiet but listening intently.

"Excellent. Hard work is critical to be successful. Do you have any hobbies?"

"I love theater. My cousin and I would go to the shut-down movie theater in Scipio, where we would rummage through old ticket stubs and jump on stage and pretend to perform in front of an audience."

"Do you hunt?" one of the brothers asked.

"No. One time my brother took me to shoot jackrabbits, but it didn't take. I usually tried to miss; I just felt bad for them," he admitted.

Mitch didn't have to be Sherlock Holmes to know he wasn't earning himself any style points. Animal heads hung on the walls in the living room and inside the garage. Pheasant, buffalo, king salmon, deer, elk, and various animal pelts hung on display. Sonja's family members weren't casual hunters. Many of their kills were from exotic hunts in Alaska, Africa, and Mongolia.

"What'd you get on the ACT?" Her dad continued the intense questioning.

"I never took it," Mitch replied.

"But you're going to BYU?" Her mom leaned forward.

"I didn't need to take it. I transferred from a community college."

"Do you like sports?" a different brother asked.

"I watch a little college football."

"And what's your GPA?" her dad asked, crossing his legs.

"I have a 3.2 GPA, which is honestly a huge improvement from high school," he answered matter-of-factly.

"Any extracurricular activities, clubs, or something to save the résumé?" her dad continued.

"My senior year, my family moved from rural central California to Texas, where I tried out for school plays. I played Brian in *The Shadow Box* and won an acting award, recognizing me as one of Texas's best high school actors."

"I don't advise you use high school accomplishments on a graduate school application. Doesn't look good. Anything else?"

"Not really." Mitch had never talked about his résumé with anyone before.

"Well, what are you planning to do professionally?" her dad asked.

"I'm thinking of being a history professor," he said.

Mitch's decision to be a history professor was driven largely by the fact that during high school, history was one of the only classes in which he'd gotten an A (actually an A-), and so he reasoned he must be good at it.

Mitch wasn't offended by their questions. It was clear that academic and professional achievements were simply frequent topics of conversation among the family, especially if someone was dating one of the children.

Mitch sat forward. "I need to head home to study, but thanks for having me over," he said as he got up to leave. Sonja followed him out and walked him to his car.

"Well, what'd you think?" she excitedly asked.

"I think you have a very nice family, but I think they question your choice in men." He managed a smile.

"Well, *my* choice in men is all that matters." She smiled back.

CHAPTER 5

The Eight-Date Wait

Mitch wanted to kiss Sonja, but he promised his sister months ago that he would go slower in his dating relationships. Her advice wasn't aimed at Sonja, but she noticed a lot of Mitch's relationships started strong and ended quickly. He would argue that if he went slow, it would take twice as long to find out if a girl was wrong for him, but despite his arguing, he conceded his sister may be right. He decided that with Sonja, it would be different.

One of Mitch's roommates swore by the "eight-date wait" method. His roommate suggested Mitch try it by not kissing Sonja until their eighth date. It just so happened that the BYU girl's choice dance would be their eighth date.

Sonja had appeared in one of Mitch's history classes when his professor turned the time over to her. She stood in front of the entire class as she confidently read a poem she wrote from a sheet of paper that asked him to the dance. The class clapped when she finished, and Mitch admired her tenacity. He walked to the front of the room to officially accept her invitation.

About twenty minutes into the dance, a slow song came on, and Mitch knew this might be his moment. Feeling bold as they swayed along with a roomful of people, he pulled her in close for a kiss. As he leaned in, Sonja unexpectedly smiled, and he ended up kissing her teeth.

"Did you just try to kiss me?" She laughed.

"Yes."

"After all this time I've been waiting for you to kiss me, you do it on the dance floor in front of hundreds of people?" She shook her head with a grin.

"I can do better." He pulled her back into his chest, and the room faded away. Having her in his arms felt natural, like she belonged there. He kissed her, this time on the lips, and she kissed him right back. "The eight-date wait was well worth it." He softly said, pressing his forehead to hers.

She paused and looked at him. "Are you serious? The eight-date wait? I was starting to think you didn't like me!" She punched him in the arm.

They were an unlikely pair, but they fell in love, each seeing something priceless in the other.

On a winter afternoon, Mitch drove Sonja up Provo Canyon to Aspen Grove; they were holding hands, listening to "Your Song" by Elton John as the snow gently fell. He looked over at her and thought, *I can't imagine life without her*. He had never felt that way about anyone he had dated. Sonja felt like his other half. All the stupid, clichéd things people say about love really did feel true. He had found his match.

Mitch parked the car in the snow. The wind whistled outside as he stroked his thumb across the back of Sonja's hand. "I don't see this ending," he softly said.

There was a silence as both Mitch and Sonja reflected on what he had just said. She kept her gaze on his hand clasped around hers.

"I know," she breathed.

"So, wait, are you saying you think we're going to get married?"

She lifted her eyes and firmly held his gaze. "Yes."

When he was with her, he felt the same peace and warmth

he felt at moments when he was completely centered, watching the sunrise through the mountains—when the reds and oranges swelled in the sky and the quaking aspen trees reminded him how simple and good life can be. With Sonja, it was the same. She was his own personal, constant alpenglow, and he wanted to feel this way forever. She had brushed a breeze through his life that made him feel alive and secure.

He grabbed her small, cold hands and pressed them to his lips. "If I've only been sure about one thing in my whole life, it's that I want to marry you."

"I feel the same way," she beamed, head held high.

White flurries danced behind her, and all he could think was, *She's going to be my wife.*

CHAPTER 6

Full Disclosure

Mitch came home as his parents were making dinner and told them that he and Sonja were getting married. The feelings he felt toward her were big and bright, and the energy was so contagious, his parents could only be excited for them.

And then Sonja told her family …

The phone rang in Mitch's apartment, and it was Sonja's father, David.

"I'd like you to meet with me today—now," he said in his large, intimidating voice. "Can you come over?"

"Sure, I'll be right over," Mitch quickly responded.

Had he made a miscalculation in not discussing his intentions with her dad before they had decided to get married? He didn't think getting a father's approval was a thing anymore.

Sonja's dad pleasantly greeted him at the front door. "Let's go for a drive."

Mitch anticipated a brief discussion in his study, but no such luck. Instead, he was treated to a lengthy four-hour car ride and asked questions that felt more suited for someone seeking high-level government clearance.

"Have you ever done drugs?" he asked, pulling out of the driveway, wasting no time.

"No," Mitch answered.

"Drunk alcohol?" he asked without a pause.

"No."

"Do you have any debts?"

"Nope."

"Any past indiscretions with former girlfriends?"

"No."

The questions got intensely personal. Mitch figured that to object to any of the questions wouldn't help his cause, so he did his best to continue answering them as they drove through Hobble Creek Canyon. It was the longest single interview Mitch had ever had—then and since.

"What are your parents like?" David asked.

"They're hardworking people who value their family and their faith, and most importantly, they *love* Sonja." He made sure to emphasize this last point. David just nodded.

All Mitch could think was, *When will this be over?*

"What's your birth order?" David continued to fire away.

"Fifth," Mitch replied.

"Ah, just like Sonja. What do your siblings do professionally?"

"My brothers have always been interested in business and work mostly in advertising and banking."

Mitch quickly learned David's aim was to leave no stone unturned and make sure he knew *exactly* what his daughter was getting herself into.

"Now, most importantly, tell me your career plan. In detail." David kept one eye on the road and one eye on Mitch as he got ready to listen.

"After I graduate from college, I want to go to graduate school. I'm thinking about being a history professor, but I'm still not 100 percent sure," Mitch answered.

"That's fine; still a lot of time to decide on a profession." David nodded. "You'll have to finish raising Sonja." He jumped topics. "I could only get her so far."

Mitch's questioning appeared to be over. Now David wanted to make sure Mitch knew *everything* he should before marrying his daughter. David broadcasted his worries about Sonja, and Mitch felt like it was a disclaimer or informed consent, so that no matter what happened, he had been informed.

"She's very idealistic. She had Cabbage Patch tea parties with her friends at seventeen!" David's facial expressions indicated his own disbelief. He kept his eyes on the road as he chewed a toothpick. "I don't always understand her. She would come home from high school and ask me, 'Why is life so hard?' I was confused because she had friends, good grades, traveled abroad, dated lots, and was a popular cheerleader. But as a teenager she always seemed to struggle with normal, day-to-day life."

He rolled down the window and continued his lecture. "I worry that Sonja has such high standards for herself that she'll work herself mercilessly. I remember her doing ballet until her feet bled. She has such a streak of obsessive-compulsive in her that things need to be a certain way."

Mitch was young and didn't have the experience to know that some of these observations were David's way of noting that red flags existed. Her dad left little breathing room for comments or follow-up questions as he passionately went on to philosophize about marriage, life, and child-rearing. Toward the end of one of his long reflections about Sonja's upbringing and his life philosophies, he looked over at Mitch and smirked.

"You passed." David's large hand gripped Mitch's shoulder.

Mitch let out a large breath, mostly relieved that the car ride was over. "Good. That's a relief." Mitch smiled back.

From that car ride on, David was a supporter and advocate of their relationship. Mitch was grateful to have an ally, and he felt David's approval and acceptance.

Sonja and Mitch came from two very different traditions when it came to dating. Mitch's parents and siblings had all gotten engaged within two months of dating the person they would marry. When they knew, they knew. Sonja's family, on the other hand, took much more time to study their choice, and some of her siblings had known their spouses for years before getting engaged. Sonja and Mitch's quick engagement created concern and conflict for many of Sonja's family members.

As the wedding date was set and inched closer, her mother and some family members still tried to dissuade Sonja from the engagement. It caused Sonja a lot of distress, and she started wavering. Mitch and Sonja had several long talks during their engagement, when she got confused by the many voices giving her advice.

"Do you love me?" Mitch asked.

"Yes!" She grabbed his hands, pained that it would ever be a question.

"And do you want to spend the rest of your life with me?" He looked into her eyes.

"Of course! Nothing would make me happier. But my mom …" She started crying again.

"Have you personally felt any hesitations about getting married?" He tried to keep her focused on her feelings, not others' opinions.

"No. Not at all. But my family …" She sobbed.

"Everyone wants their family's approval. I understand that. But I'm not going to take someone to the altar kicking and screaming. So, I want you to be committed to whatever decision you make," he said.

"I want to marry you." She took Mitch's hand and placed a small kiss in his palm. "I love you. I want you to be my future."

Her mother's disapproval of the match and timing continued to be extremely hard for Sonja. Even on the day of their wedding, her mom let her know, "It's still not too late to call it off." But it didn't stop them from getting married.

On March 6, 1992, Sonja and Mitch got married in their church's temple. It was decorated in all white with hanging crystal light fixtures, marble, stained-glass windows, and gilded gold mirrors. In the LDS religion, getting married in the temple meant you weren't only sealed together in this earth life but in the life after as well. It wasn't "till death do us part"; it was an eternal marriage that lasted into heaven forever. Sonja was dressed in all white with her black hair tied up with two loose strands around her face. Mitch couldn't take his eyes off her.

After the temple ceremony, they had a reception at Sonja's family mansion. They stood in their wedding receiving line, greeting guests. Mitch and Sonja cut their wedding cake, which was decorated with fresh flowers. After chatting with friends and family, they got ready to say their goodbyes. Sonja climbed into the car in her lace wedding dress, and Mitch was still in his tuxedo. As they drove off, cans rattled behind the car. The cheering crowd faded from view, and soon it was just Mitch and Sonja with hands clasped tight.

"I'm so excited to do life with you," Mitch beamed as he kissed the back of Sonja's hand.

"Me too. All of it." Sonja smiled back.

CHAPTER 7

The Train

"We're not going anywhere today, are we?" Mitch asked as Sonja spent another hour in front of the mirror, contemplating blouses.

"Nope." She shook her hips to the James Taylor CD playing.

She then slipped a white lacy blouse over her head and buttoned up the high collar that ended just at her jawline.

"Then what're you getting ready for?" he asked.

"Just life. I enjoy it." She curled the last strand of hair. "Fashion is my thing. I coordinate my hairstyles with my outfits. I like achieving a certain look each day. Anyone who really knows me could tell you that." She looked back at him.

"Six weeks into marriage, and I'm learning all the secrets you failed to divulge in courtship." He pulled her waist against him. "Dance with me," he said.

"If you insist." She laughed, draping her wrists over his neck. She looked too good to belong in their run-down apartment, like a china doll in a pawn shop.

Many people had told them how hard the first year of marriage could be, but their first year together felt light and effortless. Sonja and Mitch just seemed to fit. They were that nauseatingly chummy couple that didn't have much to fight about and were affectionate in public.

Sonja strutted into the kitchen with her arms full of brochures she had collected from the career center. "Now, are you ready to career plan?" Sonja asked, laying a stack on the kitchen table.

"I don't know. I'm still not completely sure I want to be a history professor." He sat looking at the brochures.

Even despite the ways they were polar opposites, which were many, they melded. Sonja was an amazing coach, and it was clear mapping out a career came as easily to her as breathing, whereas Mitch had never learned how to study for a test or map anything further out than two weeks ahead. He was like a cork bobbing along the stream—his major skills were his optimism, a good sense of humor, and the ability to create rapport with people. Unfortunately for him, these wouldn't help him get into graduate school.

"Let's write down a bunch of different careers you would be interested in." Sonja sat down energetically, getting ready to take notes. "Then you can talk to people in those professions, to see what they do every day. I think you should ask if you could shadow them at work, to make sure you would be happy doing that job," she suggested.

"That sounds like a good idea."

"Once you figure out what career path you want to take, we can look into that field and figure out what GPA and internship you'd need to get into the right graduate school program."

Sonja took what he wanted to do seriously. In her eyes, every career was a viable option. Mitch remembered attending a Utah Jazz game with her. They watched basketball players squeak across the glossy court, while a man rattled off behind them about how much fun being a professional basketball player would be. Sonja quickly grabbed Mitch's arm. "You should do that!" she said, as if she'd had a brilliant moment of insight. She was a dreamer in every sense of the word.

Although it was completely unrealistic, the fact that she believed he could be an NBA player was incredibly endearing to him. He loved her complete belief in him.

After applying for several summer internships, Mitch ended up with one in Washington, DC, working in the National Archives.

He abstracted Civil War veterans' pension records to find out why some lived longer than others. He looked at income, stress, nutrition, and battle injuries. It introduced him to epidemiology, the study of disease in populations. The study was headed by Dr. Robert Fogel, an economic historian from the University of Chicago, who had won the Nobel Prize in Economics that year. During this internship, Mitch realized he was more interested in the public health aspects of the study than the history aspects.

After months of researching different careers—professor, lawyer, doctor, dentist, banker, accountant—Mitch decided on healthcare administration. To apply, he would need to take the Graduate Management Admission Test (GMAT), and Sonja wasted no time signing him up for a test-prep course with Kaplan.

Mitch flipped the next page in his glossy-papered textbook and continued reading. He rubbed his temples as hour five of studying set in.

Sonja burst through the front door. "Look what I brought you!" she said holding a fishbowl and bags from the pet store.

"What in the world?" He looked at her, confused.

He hadn't asked for a pet. Water sloshed side to side as she walked her way over to him and set the fishbowl on the table. Mitch moved his textbook a few inches to avoid the small splash of water.

"What's this?" He looked into the bowl of swimming goldfish and a tiny frog.

"Study buddies," Sonja proudly said. "You have so much studying ahead of you, with the GMAT and keeping your grades up, so I wanted to send you reinforcements." She tapped the glass, and their scales flashed metallic shades of orange. "These little guys will be here with you for every minute of your studying. You won't ever have to do it alone."

"I love them. They look like a hardy crew." He smiled at the fish.

"The hardiest." She kissed him.

Mitch applied to over fifteen graduate schools, even the top five, which he doubted he could get into, but Sonja was convinced they were all real possibilities. After waiting to hear back for months, he realized she was right when he checked their mailbox.

"I got invited to interview with the University of Michigan!" he yelled to Sonja, holding his letter. "The number one school in health-care administration," he said to himself, hoping it would feel more real.

"Oh my gosh! When's the interview?" Sonja threw her arms around him.

"Wait." He set her down. "How will we afford the airfare to get there?" His stomach dropped.

"Let's see if there's a cheaper way to get there; maybe you could take the train?" Sonja suggested.

"That would take days."

"That's okay." She shrugged. "Whatever gets you there."

That night, Mitch bought a train ticket from Provo, Utah, to Ann Arbor, Michigan, and spent the whole night visualizing how the interview would go. He looked over at the fish tank on the table and smiled. "We did it," he whispered.

Mitch spent the train ride there practicing interview questions for two days straight. He had a hard time sleeping at night because of nerves and ended up giving himself a painful canker sore because of stress. He continually prayed to God that if he would just help him get accepted to a good graduate school, he would work his hardest to be successful.

Snow flurries blew as he walked across the University of Michigan campus to his interview. He had a coat that was far too light to be useful. Mitch walked into the School of Public Health and took a seat in the lobby. The department chair came out to escort him into his office.

"Wow, you took a train here!" He warmly smiled at Mitch. Mitch was uncomfortable that the secretary had let him know that he was too poor to fly.

After his interview, the school committee informed him they wanted students who'd take their time at the school seriously and stated that they liked not only his résumé but also his tenacity. They were very impressed that he had spent four days on a train round trip just for an interview. He had never thought he stood a chance of getting into their program, but of course, when he got his acceptance letter to the University of Michigan several weeks later, Sonja knew he had had it in him all along. She was a force of nature, a woman who believed things into existence.

CHAPTER 8

Josephine

Ypsilanti, Michigan
October 2, 1994

The first year of graduate school, Sonja delivered a baby girl, Rachael Lynne Wasden. Meeting his daughter for the first time, Mitch felt that immediate shift, from life being all about you to it being completely about someone else who depended on you. From the moment he held Rachael in his arms, she had his heart, and Mitch knew family was what life was really all about.

Sonja dressed Rachael in pink PJs she got at a garage sale and put a tiny pink bow glued on what little hair she had with corn syrup. Sonja's greatest dream was to be a mother. That had been the only career she ever wanted. While she and Mitch were dating, he remembered in the corner of Sonja's bedroom was a stack of children's books and baby clothes she had been collecting since she was twelve years old.

He felt incredibly nervous taking Rachael home. Mitch couldn't believe the nurses and doctors were letting them take a baby home without even an interview. To drive a car, you had to study and pass a test, but the hospital was letting them take a tiny new life home without verifying they knew how to be fit parents. He prayed he would never let her down.

After the first year of graduate school, Mitch got a summer internship at Henry Ford Hospital in Detroit, Michigan. To be closer to his internship, Mitch and Sonja moved out of student housing and moved in with Josephine, a ninety-eight-year-old blind woman. They took care of her, and in return, they lived rent free and were paid fifty dollars a week. Sonja, Mitch, and their nine-month-old daughter slept in the attic along with all of Josephine's stored possessions. There were a lot of things Josephine's daughter didn't disclose when hiring them, like the fact that her mom was incontinent and often had accidents in the bed in the middle of the night, or that the house had no air-conditioning.

"Sonja!" Josephine yelled in the middle of the night.

What did we just sign up for? Mitch thought as he turned over on his side and shook Sonja's arm to wake her up.

"She's calling you again," he whispered, eyes closed.

"Sonja, quick!" Josephine yelled again.

The bed creaked as Sonja tiredly stood up and walked down the steep and unusually tiny stairs down to the main floor. Mitch lay with Rachael in the bed while Sonja went down to bathe Josephine.

That morning, Mitch carried Rachael into the kitchen. "Good morning," he greeted Josephine.

"Morning!" Josephine said over her TV show. Even though she couldn't see, she loved sitting by her TV and listening to the programs.

Sonja stopped the blender. Josephine had stomach issues, which meant all her food needed to be blended. "Are we still going to the mall?" Sonja asked, pushing a sweaty strand of hair out of her face.

"Uh, yeah. I can't do another day without AC." Mitch sighed.

Being in a humid attic in July with no AC quickly felt oppressive. The heat was so unbearable that they escaped to the mall for just an hour to walk around in the cool air.

"Get my hair!" Josephine yelled.

"Okay." Sonja poured the blended food in a bowl and went into Josephine's bedroom to get the hair. She brought out the long braid wrapped in newspaper and set it in Josephine's hands. Her frail fingers pulled the newspaper back and felt for the braid.

"It was my greatest beauty." Josephine smiled, touching the bright-red hair.

"It's beautiful," Sonja always agreed. Josephine had cut her hair off when she was in her twenties, which meant that braid was *seventy* years old. But Mitch tried not to think about that.

Mitch loved his internship and felt excited he was learning valuable skills to be successful in his career. He called Sonja every day at lunch to check in with her to see how she and Rachael were doing. And every day her answer was the same: "Not good." It was unlike her to be "not good" day after day. She was so energetic and vivacious that seeing her sad was unusual.

At breakfast the next morning, Sonja was still in a slump. "I feel sad again," Sonja cried.

"Why?" He spooned applesauce into Rachael's mouth.

Mitch had grown up surrounded by four brothers and a rarely emotional sister and mother, so he was largely unprepared to handle Sonja's tears.

"I just am. This whole week, I've felt down and burst into tears randomly." She looked out the window. "I don't know why."

"I think I do. You're stuck in a house with a nine-month-old baby and ninety-eight-year-old woman who both need to be changed, fed, and entertained. Your feelings make perfect sense."

"They do?" She looked up at him.

"Yeah. While I'm gone, you're doing so much to take care of Rachael and Josephine. This would be hard for anyone."

Mitch felt confident Sonja's mood would lift once the summer internship was over and they were back to having their own space.

CHAPTER 9

Sonja Slipping Away

After the internship, Mitch, Sonja, and Rachael moved back to Ann Arbor to finish Mitch's second year of graduate school, where they received a big surprise. Sonja was pregnant with baby number two. They moved into a studio apartment with one large room and a closet of a bathroom, but compared to Josephine's attic, it was spacious.

Sonja tiredly pushed the grocery cart through the store, while Mitch entertained Rachael with goofy faces as he tickled her. He adored his daughter's laughter, and she most definitely had her daddy wrapped around her tiny finger.

"We have forty-five dollars for groceries this week," Mitch said.

"We need more diapers," Sonja let him know.

Mitch pointed to a clearance box that looked like it had been opened and then taped closed as he kissed Rachael's chubby cheeks.

"And Rachael needs a new pacifier; she lost hers." Sonja added one to the cart. "But don't worry; I'll still keep looking for it."

They passed the produce section of the store, and Sonja flocked to the cartons of fresh berries.

"Don't worry; I'm just looking," she promised him.

"One day." He smiled at Sonja.

"One day," she repeated.

Their simple diet didn't bother Mitch, but he knew it was hard for Sonja to not have better food. When he was growing up, his mom served the family cracked-wheat cereal for breakfast with milk from the cows they hand milked each morning. At school, Mitch's lunches consisted of his mom's homemade bread, which fell apart easily, with peanut butter and honey. His mother had memorized the bread recipe but often forgot the salt. Food was nothing more than fuel to Mitch, but to Sonja it was a source of joy.

That night, after Rachael was in bed, Mitch sat at the kitchen table, eating chips and salsa while Sonja munched on saltine crackers and sipped 7UP, which did little to stop her from throwing up. Sonja was already in a fragile state, but Mitch couldn't put off the bad news any longer.

"We're short on money," he cautiously got out.

They were paying for Mitch's graduate program and living expenses through a partial scholarship, student loans, and Mitch's part-time job, yet they were still coming up short because Sonja became so sick with this pregnancy that she couldn't work.

"Okay." Sonja sipped her 7UP.

"So, we'll need to sell the car to pay for rent." He pinched the back of his neck.

"Then how will you go to school? Or work? That's our only car!" Sonja started to panic.

"We'll figure it out. I can walk to school and ask some people if I can carpool to work. It's only for another semester; after I graduate, I'll have a job, and it'll be fine," he reassured her.

"I guess," she said, unconvinced.

"Hold on; your dad's calling." Mitch answered the phone.

During their time in graduate school, Sonja's dad was going through a multiyear lawsuit with the federal government and would often call to give updates.

"Now the government has charged me with thirty-four counts of mail fraud and money laundering! Can you believe that!" David launched into the details.

The phone call was to inform them that because of the financial drain of the lawsuit and the high cost of the upkeep of their home and Appaloosa ranch, they needed all the kids to pitch in and help. The proposed solution was to have each family member take out credit cards in their name and send as much cash as possible to David. Mitch hung up and turned to Sonja, baffled as he explained the situation.

"Your dad wants us to take out credit cards and send him the money," Mitch said, stunned.

"Well, don't worry, we're not doing that." She sighed tensely.

"Sonja, are you worried about him? With the lawsuits and the spending?"

"That's just my dad; he's always been in the middle of battles. Don't worry too much about it; he always comes through."

"Your dad's whole situation just stresses me out." Mitch ran a hand through his hair. "I could never be calm if that were my life."

"Then be grateful we're only poor." Sonja kissed him on her way to bed.

Mitch sold their Chevy Nova for two grand. Several months later, his parents, who had just bought a new car, gave them their old Honda Accord with over two hundred thousand miles on it. It was reliable and felt like manna from heaven.

Mitch continued working hard on his schoolwork and research-assistant job. He began applying for healthcare fellowships all while taking on more responsibilities at home.

Sonja was often lying in bed trying to escape life through sleep. Mitch did all the cleaning and cooking, and when he came home from school, he took care of Rachael.

Sonja had lost interest in the things she normally loved, like painting, nature walks, or socializing with friends. Instead, she would lie on the floor, watching Rachael play with her toys. Mitch came home each day to find Sonja slumped somewhere in the apartment with little energy to talk. What to eat for dinner seemed a too-difficult decision for her to make, so he stopped asking and just made them food every night. She seemed to cry nonstop. Confidence wasn't something he struggled with, so when Sonja started asking him daily how good of a mother, wife, or person she was, it got exhausting to provide the same validations dozens of times per day.

Months passed, and Mitch felt like he was watching a radiant flower wilt. Despite doing his best to take care of her, nothing seemed to revive her. Her roots were withering, and he had no clue how to water them.

She was no longer the person he had married. Still, he remained certain that her distressing emotions were temporary, the result of a difficult pregnancy and their current financial situation, unaware of the true battle being waged against her.

CHAPTER 10

A Religious Divide

Summer 1996

Mitch excitedly handed Sonja his offer letter for a prestigious postgraduate fellowship with Lovelace Health System in Albuquerque.

"Thirty thousand dollars a year, baby!" He picked up Rachael and swung her around.

"Mitch, this is incredible; finally, we have a job!" Sonja clasped her mouth. "We will never be broke again!" she squealed, flashing the offer letter at him like their own victory flag.

⸺✢✢⸺

Mitch, Sonja, and Rachael made the trek from Ann Arbor to Albuquerque in a U-Haul with their Honda Accord in tow. Their external circumstances had improved dramatically. Mitch had a good-paying job, they had a healthy daughter, with another baby on the way, their apartment had a pool, and the sun shone almost every day in Albuquerque. Before work in the morning, Mitch would open the front door, smell the grass, and listen to the sprinklers. He felt immediate happiness and gratitude.

That happiness grew tenfold on October 23, 1996, when Sonja delivered an almost-ten-pound boy in the same hospital where

Mitch worked. They named their second child Alexander Mitchell Wasden.

Yet Sonja did not feel the joy Mitch was experiencing. As she inexplicably worsened, Mitch realized that logic wasn't going to make Sonja's painful emotions disappear, and he made a doctor's appointment.

"What are your symptoms?" The doctor scooted his rolling stool over to Sonja.

"I have a hard time getting out of bed. I'm just sad. But nothing sad has happened. I have lost interest in life. My emotions are painful. Does that make sense?" Sonja explained.

"This is very common after pregnancy. No need for concern," the doctor assured her.

"I felt like this before I got pregnant too, though. It's just been getting worse with time," she quickly added.

"Well, with everything you've told me, I feel confident that you're experiencing depression. I'll prescribe you Zoloft, and let's see if that helps." He clicked his pen and put it back in his pocket.

"You think the medicine will fix it?" Mitch asked eagerly.

"Not all at once, but it should gradually start to help. We will see you back in two months." The doctor shook their hands before leaving.

Mitch let out a sigh of relief. All he wanted was his vivacious Sonja back. He paid extra-close attention to Sonja's moods over the next few months and noticed more moments when her mood seemed to lift. She laughed more; she got out of bed a little more. At least he thought so—perhaps he was just desperately looking for any sign of improvement. The only big change Mitch noticed in Sonja was her religious habits.

"I'll pray tonight." Mitch knelt next to her as she lay on the bed.

"Please don't." She sighed.

Sonja had spent so many nights praying and pleading for relief from her emotional pain that to do it again could cause a kind of posttraumatic stress for her. Similar to the conditioned response of Pavlov's dog, when Sonja knelt to pray, she felt abandonment from a God who didn't step in and relieve her pain. While Mitch and Sonja were the same religion, it felt like a two-faith household.

"Okay, I'll just pray in my head. Do you want me to read a scripture to you tonight?" he asked cautiously.

"I can't handle reading about wars, sins, and the devil anymore. It freaks me out." She turned on her side. "Scripture stories are so depressing."

When Mitch first married Sonja, they would pray and read scriptures together every night, but now that all stopped. He'd never conceived that his marriage would lack the spiritual dimensions he had seen in his parents' marriage. Mitch grew up in a traditional Christian home that taught praying, church attendance, and reading the scriptures brought peace and comfort. But those solutions weren't working for Sonja. She began to question where she could turn for peace if the things she had practiced since childhood no longer worked.

At church, she used to cheerfully sing hymns, but that had since morphed into an expressionless staring contest with the podium. Sonja now spent church meetings leaning against Mitch's shoulder, sleeping.

"I'm tired of sitting in church Sunday after Sunday, listening to members talk about the peace and joy the gospel brings into their lives, when all I experience is pain," Sonja said one evening.

"I know you feel out of place at church, but God sees you trying. That's enough," Mitch said, trying to comfort her as he attempted to hold her hand. She pulled her hand away and began to cry.

"It's just the stronger I push myself toward God, the more it hurts when I can't feel his soft presence."

"He is there for you, I promise," he tenderly said.

"I'm trying to be a faithful Christian, but I don't feel what other people are feeling. In fact, I feel more like the sinners in that lake of fire and brimstone. I feel the wrath of hell, and I don't know what I did to deserve it," she said, defeated.

Mitch grasped for something wise or impactful to say but came up short. "Sony, I have no answer for why you are in pain. I know a lot of things, but I don't know that. We can choose to believe in God instead of viewing the pain as proof that there is no higher being at all."

Sonja looked up. "What I'm learning is, God is okay letting us suffer."

CHAPTER 11

The Wild Ride

"We're going to New Orleans. I feel it," Sonja declared excitedly as they ate their Saturday breakfast.

"Are you psychic?" Mitch teased.

She'd been going on like this for months, absolutely convinced they were moving to New Orleans. Mitch's former boss at Lovelace Hospital in Albuquerque, New Mexico, Dr. Robert Turner, had taken a new job in New Orleans as the chief medical officer of the Ochsner Health System. They had worked well together, running several rural health clinics throughout New Mexico, and he told Mitch he would keep him in mind if a job became available. But other than that small detail, they had no reason to believe they were going there too.

"I'm telling you—you have the connection; the opportunity is coming. Get ready, Mitch." Sonja happily ate another piece of bacon. Mitch was just relieved the depression medicine seemed to be working.

"Mom, we need more icing!" Rachael complained.

Rachael and Alex sat at the kitchen table frosting large car sponges with shaving cream. "What are you guys making?" Mitch asked.

"I'm decorating a wedding cake." Rachael dug her hands in a tower of shaving cream.

Alex pressed his little thumb on top the shaving cream can, and short foam strands sputtered out onto the kitchen table.

"Your cake is beautiful," Sonja said, bringing over another can. Rachael swept a butter knife across the top of the sponge.

Alex held out his sponge covered in shaving cream to Mitch.

Mitch pretended to eat a piece of cake. "Mmm, lemon meringue. My favorite!"

"I had another great idea!" Sonja threw her hand on his shoulder.

"For your *Wrap It Up* book?" he asked, looking over at the hundreds of colorfully wrapped boxes stacked in the corner of their family room. Sonja had the idea to create a picture book displaying all the different ways to wrap gifts. The boxes were empty, but each had tightly pressed corners, different paper themes, and styles of bows.

"No, no. That project is almost done. I just need to photograph some more bows. This is a new idea," Sonja said, upbeat.

"When do we get to open the gifts?" Rachael asked again for the hundredth time.

"Soon." Sonja kissed her cheek.

"Well, let's hear it," Mitch said, opening a box of Cheez-Its.

"I've invented something." Sonja bit her lip excitedly. "I was vacuuming the house and kept thinking about how I hate running into baseboards and furniture with the vacuum head. Even when you're careful, the vacuum scratches and marks stuff up." She paused to make sure Mitch was following her.

"Yeah. So, what's the invention?"

"Vacuum Bra," she beamed.

"What?" Mitch about choked on a Cheez-It, trying not to laugh.

"It's a cushioned cover you put on the front of your vacuum to stop the corners from scraping things. It's so needed and so practical."

"That's actually not a bad idea." Mitch nodded.

"I don't know how I come up with all these ideas. They just come to me!" she said as if in disbelief. "The only problem is—"

She leaned over the counter. "I don't have enough time in the day to focus on *all* my interests."

"That's a good problem to have." Mitch smiled at her energy. "I love seeing you happy." He kissed her forehead, blissfully unaware that what appeared to him as a joyful display of positive energy was actually the beginning signs of a manic episode—the first of many to come.

CHAPTER 12

Risking It All

Mandeville, Louisiana
1998

Several months later, when Mitch got the call from Dr. Turner, offering him the job of director of Ochsner's primary care clinics, Sonja wasn't even shocked. She just said, "Told you so."

Though Mitch worked in New Orleans, they lived in the suburb of Mandeville, Louisiana, because the housing was cheaper, the crime rate was lower, and the schools were better. It was a forty-five-minute commute to work each day across the world's longest bridge, the twenty-three-mile Lake Pontchartrain Causeway. With Mitch's new job, they had managed to save $4,800 and open a brokerage account. They invested in an S&P Index mutual fund and kept investing each month. For the first time in their lives, they had accumulated some savings.

Mitch got the mail on a hot Saturday in August and saw a credit card statement he didn't recognize. When he opened it, to his shock, he saw his name on the credit card alongside a $10,000 balance. He ran in the house to show Sonja; he was sure they had been the victims of identity theft.

"Daddy, look at my painting!" Rachael begged.

"Looking great," he said quickly as he glanced at her picture, preoccupied with his panic.

"All done," Alex said, stepping away from his watercolor painting.

"Sonja! Someone's opened up a credit card in my name!" Mitch showed her the paper.

Her eyes darted from one line to another and then went back to sporadically rinsing and drying paintbrushes. "Love that dragon!" Sonja said to Alex, ignoring Mitch.

"*Daddddd*," Rachael sang, wanting Mitch's attention.

"Hold on, Rach." Mitch sighed. "Look at the balance." He pointed to the numbers.

Sonja turned off the sink. "Okay, don't be mad."

"That sounds exactly like the kind of thing someone says right before their husband gets mad," Mitch said cautiously.

"Kids, why don't you go to the playroom for a bit," Sonja said as they obediently left. "I had one of my great ideas again." She got serious. "But it didn't go the way I planned."

"What?"

"I lost some money in the stock market."

"When did you start buying stocks?" His eyes widened in disbelief.

"People were making money in the dot-com stocks, and we were missing out! I put us in the game. And maybe that was risky, but if our friends are capable of winning in the stock market, then so are we." She raised a tight fist.

"Sonja, this is our money; you can't make decisions like that without telling me," he said in complete shock.

"Maybe some of my ideas come at a cost, but all important things involve risk. We need to take *massive* action!" She spoke as if their living room was an auditorium for motivational speakers and she was tonight's keynoter. "If you do what you've always done, you'll get what you've always gotten."

"Are you trying to quote Tony Robbins?" Mitch sighed. "Sonja, just tell me *how much* money we lost."

"I'm not totally sure. But we can turn it around. Look, every problem is a gift, and without problems, we wouldn't grow."

"*Stop* quoting Tony Robbins! Just how—how did this happen?" He closed his eyes.

"I called a stockbroker, who told me about some stocks that were going up, so I sold our mutual fund to buy those stocks. It turned out he was right—the stock went way up, and all of a sudden, we had over nine thousand dollars. It almost doubled our money!" She cheered, reliving the moment. "I've been nervous to tell you but also excited because this stockbroker knew what he was doing." She then blurted, "I can't explain it. It just felt right! Like I *knew in my bones* we couldn't lose."

Mitch interrupted her. "But we did lose ..." He took a big breath, suddenly losing his patience. "So, how'd we go from having $9,000 to *owing* $10,000?" he screamed.

"If we borrowed money, we could make more, so I took out some credit cards to get cash advances and used that to buy more stock. I got an introductory rate, where we didn't have to pay interest for six months, which would give us time to make money. Then the stockbroker told me about this thing where I could buy stock on the margin and use our existing stock as collateral to buy other stocks."

She spoke about each detail of the process like it had been clever, like she not only had the gumption but courage to pull this off. Mitch couldn't believe what he was hearing.

"I can't trust you." He clenched his jaw.

"What?" Sonja jolted back like the shot had come out of left field.

"You're being just like your dad. Risking everything to win big or lose it all!" he snapped.

"*That* is not true." Sonja held a firm finger at him. "I was being savvy. The outcome was out of my control."

"How many credit cards did you take out?" he asked coldly.

"I don't remember," she scoffed.

"Give me the credit cards and just ... go. I need you to leave so I can figure this out," he said, feeling as if he were living in some alternate reality.

Sonja's eyes finally looked up to meet his. "Okay, I'm sorry. I thought I was helping," she said as tears started to roll down her cheeks.

"I need you to go—really, just go," he said, shifting his gaze to the ground. He couldn't process anything until he knew how financially at risk they were.

Mitch stayed up that night on the phone with six credit card companies.

"Can you hold?" the agent asked for the third time.

"Yes," he sighed, tracing "$30,000" several shades darker as anger, fury, and shock filled him. An agent from another credit card company tried calling back. Mitch hung up and answered the new call.

"Sorry for the wait; did you need your outstanding balance?" the agent said.

"Yes, please; how much is on the card?" He rushed him along.

"The total is $18,000."

He let out an audible gasp, like he had been punched in the gut. He wrote down "$18,000," adding it to already existing thirty. Surely there couldn't be much more. He had to believe that.

He called the last credit card company and waited on hold. Again. He was desperately trying to grasp the situation, but writing down numbers on paper wasn't helping him.

"Hello, Mitch?" The agent finally cut through the on-hold music.

"Yes?" He picked up the pen, hoping he wouldn't need it.

"The total amount charged was …" She paused. "$32,000." He snapped the pen in half and ink spilled everywhere; $80,000.

He sat on the wood floor of their family room late that evening, after everyone had gone to bed, and for the first time since he was twelve years old, he cried. Mitch had never been an emotional person. He ruled most of his life through logic. He didn't even cry at his children's birth. Making him show raw emotions was like moving a boulder, and this would not be the last time that Sonja would push him to his limits.

He had no way of paying off $80,000 in credit card debt aside from the $400 a month they had been saving. Money had never been an issue in their marriage. Sonja had rarely overspent or done anything like this before. What was she thinking? She had gambled away financial resources they needed for their children. He felt a deep betrayal. With Mitch, Sonja had always been an open book. She shared her ideas and thoughts with him the moment they came to her mind, and in return he felt comfortable doing the same. They shared their souls with each other, and he couldn't figure out why she'd do this behind his back. It was the first time that deep hurt and love had coexisted in their marriage.

It was going to take years to even make a dent in this kind of debt. The next week he cashed out what little he had in his company 401(k) retirement plan to pay a small portion of his debts and went to work the next day desperate to prove himself, in hopes that he could dig his family out of this hole. There was only one way out. He needed raises, he needed promotions, and he needed bonuses.

Mitch was getting up earlier and earlier each day and staying later and later at work in hopes of getting a promotion. He only saw his kids for twenty minutes before they went to sleep but always made sure he got home in time to put them to bed.

"Daddy!" Rachael and Alex ran to the door in their PJs.

"Ready for bed?" He hugged them.

"I caught three lizards today," Rachael proudly informed him. "We spent all day making a habitat for them, but then I thought it was best to let them be free," she said, peering up at Mitch.

"I'd have to agree." Mitch nodded. "Though I'm sure your habitat was the best they'd ever seen."

Alex dragged Mitch into their bedroom. Alex was a daddy's boy, always had been. Anywhere Mitch was, Alex was also, like his shadow. Whatever Mitch said, Alex logged away as scripture.

Mitch sat down in the middle of the bed, and the kids curled up next to him like kittens.

"So, where did we leave off?" Mitch asked, reaching over to scratch their backs.

"Black Bart's traps!" Alex excitedly said with his little hands moving every which way. "Cowboy Johnny," he said trying to describe the dangerous parts. "Got away."

"That's right." Mitch smiled. "Okay. So, there he was, climbing up a tree to freedom, when he heard a sudden thump!" Mitch clapped his hands together. "Black Bart found him!"

"No!" Rachael and Alex cried out.

"But Cowboy Johnny was faster than Bart," Mitch continued. The kids' eyelids fell heavy as the story went on, and soon they were fast asleep. "Good night, cuties," he whispered, leaning over to kiss them both on their foreheads. This was Mitch's favorite part of each day.

CHAPTER 13

OCD

1999

Sonja was pregnant with their third child, and she was taking nesting to a whole new level.

"I need your highest-quality, most durable brand of paint." Sonja slapped her hands on the Home Depot counter. "Like, your *most* durable paint," she stressed.

"All right. That would be … any one of these." The Home Depot employee bent down to a shelf of paint. "They're our high-performance paint."

"Okay, I need to see a sample of each." She dug through her purse and pulled out a bottle of Soft Scrub and a dish sponge.

"Why'd you bring that?" Mitch asked, shocked but not shocked.

"I need to test their scratchability." Her serious eyes glanced up at him.

"Their scratchability?" He raised an eyebrow.

"Here are the three samples." The employee set three wooden stir sticks on the counter that had been dipped in the paint and blow-dried.

"Can you wet this?" She handed him back the sponge.

This was the part of running errands where Mitch would walk away to "browse." He knew Sonja could get locked on a task, and at times it was uncomfortable, so he just let her do her thing.

"Um, sure." The employee took her sponge and rinsed a small amount of water on it.

"Perfect." She squeezed Soft Scrub on the rough side of the sponge and scrubbed each paint sample.

Mitch came back and whispered in her ear, "For garage paint, we should really just get something cheap."

"Absolutely not. The garage has to endure the elements. Rain, snow, car oil." Her eyes widened with each thing.

"No." He laughed. "Most people buy cheap paint for their garage, if they paint their garage at all."

"I have a hard time believing that," she scoffed. "Look." She tilted one of the samples in the light. "This one has scratches."

"I don't see anything." Mitch looked at the patch of gray paint.

"Mitch, look! How do you not see that! There are little scratches all over!" She intensely rocked the sample side to side in his face. "Look at that!" Her eyes got big.

A burly customer approached the paint desk. "I need your cheapest paint. I'm just painting my garage."

Mitch looked at Sonja and mouthed, "Told you so." He grinned.

Anytime Mitch felt a tinge of happiness, their debt immediately came to mind, and any feelings of joy vanished. He could not talk to Sonja about the debt situation without her losing it. So, to keep the peace and keep her stable, he quietly made monthly payments.

One day, Mitch came home from work to a smell that burned his nostrils.

"Why do I smell bleach?" He scrunched his nose, walking into the family room.

"The carpets needed to be cleaned," Sonja stiffly said.

Instead of cleaning up the house before she ran the carpet cleaner, she had shoved everything off the carpets and onto the wood floors. There were toys, laundry, and schoolwork scattered all over the house. Mitch inspected all the carpets in the house and stormed back into the family room.

"Sonja! There are bleached spots all over the carpet," he said, exasperated.

"I put bleach in the carpet cleaner," she let him know as she stood ironing all of their pillowcases.

"You can't bleach carpet," he said, astonished she'd even tried.

"At least they're sanitized." She tightly pressed the folds on a finished pillowcase.

"Sonja, you've got to acknowledge this is not normal."

"Normal? What does that even mean?" She slammed the iron down and charged out of the room.

Mitch followed her. "You're cleaning things to the point of destroying them."

Sonja abruptly stopped, turned, and faced him, eyes blazing. "*Stop*. Just *stop*!" she screamed.

He grabbed and hugged her tight. "Please, just listen."

"I just want to die!" She began to sob.

"Sonja, what does death have to do with taking cleaning to the extreme?"

"I'm sick of life! I just want it to be over!" she cried.

Mitch gently rubbed her back and let her cry it out. The baby was due in a couple of months, and he didn't want to stress her out any more than she already was and push her over the edge. He got used to coming home to things being broken in unexplainable ways. Mitch stopped questioning and fighting Sonja about this issue because he realized nothing he said was deterring her obsession with cleaning. Mitch chose to ignore this strange behavior until it no longer could be avoided.

After Mitch's church meeting, he sat in a pew, waiting for Sonja and the kids. She was late again. As the congregation sang the second hymn, Sonja and the kids bustled into the church. As Alex and Rachael scooted into the pew next to Mitch, he noticed the back of Alex's khakis were dark and wet. *Did he have another accident?* Mitch worried. Rachael stood up to straighten her dress, which was wet too.

"Sonja, what happened to the kids?" Mitch whispered.

"What?" Sonja leaned in trying to hear him. The back of Sonja's blouse was soaked, as well as her skirt.

"Where were you?" Mitch touched her blouse as he looked at his soaked family, perplexed. It wasn't raining outside, and he couldn't piece together how all of them managed to soak only one side of their clothes.

"It's not a big deal. We'll talk after church." Sonja swatted his hand away.

After church, Mitch followed Sonja and the kids out to the parking lot. "So, are we going to talk about this now?" He stood by the van.

She got into the car, sidestepping his question. "You take the kids home in your car, and I'll meet you there."

"Sonja!" Mitch said, exhausted with her.

Sonja acted like he wasn't talking to her as she put the keys into the ignition. The ignition clicked and popped without starting. She pounded the steering wheel and cranked the key again. The car continued to whine and sputter until the engine gave out. Sonja finally acknowledged Mitch's presence.

"Ugh, can you try it?" She handed Mitch the keys. He hopped in the driver's seat and slid the key in the ignition.

"Whoa!" He pulled his back away from the seat as he felt water coming through his suit pants. He jumped out of the car. "What in the world!" He pressed his palm on the chair. "Why is the seat wet?" Water seeped out like he was pressing a filled sponge. Mitch looked around the car and noticed pools of water in the cupholders and on the floor mats. "Sonja, did you crash in a lake or something?" He looked up at her.

"No." She stayed quiet.

"What happened to the car then?" He tested all the seats, and sure enough, each one was drenched. "Why is the inside of the car wet?" he asked again.

"I quickly stopped at a car wash." She brushed past his question. "If it won't start, you can just take us all home."

"A car wash?" He looked at the inside of the car, confused. "Were the windows rolled down?" He tried piecing it together.

"Mom used the water gun and sprayed everything!" Rachael jumped in.

"My fishy crackers on the ground went *flying*! It was so cool!" Alex shouted enthusiastically at Mitch.

"You power washed the inside of the car?" Mitch asked, stunned.

"I can't have you yell at me! I already know it was a mistake!" She got defensive.

"Sonja." He sighed.

She hopped into the car, desperately turning the key one last time. "I think we can still save it."

"No." He shook his head. "It's dead."

Mitch tried to understand Sonja's impulsive behavior to power wash the inside of the car but couldn't, and frustration filled him.

On September 1, 1999, Sonja delivered a nine pound healthy boy, and they named him Lincoln. Sonja sat nursing Lincoln with her newspapers spread out on the kitchen table and a highlighter marker in one of her hands. Mitch carefully watched her as he ate his breakfast. Her new favorite pastime was collecting obituaries.

"Most of these people died in their early eighties," she informed him, highlighting people's names printed in black ink.

"Well, then you have a lot of life to live yet."

"I wish I was already eighty, then I would know I could die any day, and this life would soon just be over," she said wishfully.

"I'm glad you're not. We still need and want you around."

"I think you and the kids would be better off without me," she said matter-of-factly as she continued circling people's names who had passed away.

Mitch got up from the table and gently took her face in his hands and looked her in the eyes. "We love you, Sonja."

"I feel like earth life is God's classroom, and he decides when his students get to go home. Even though my hand is raised, pleading for him to pick me, he keeps picking other people to die. It's not fair."

It was clear to Mitch that Sonja's depression had come back full force. Her obsession with death and wanting to die deeply concerned him. In hopes of getting some help, Mitch went with her to the next doctor appointment.

"The depression medicine isn't working anymore," Mitch told the doctor.

"Sonja, tell me how you have been feeling." The doctor turned to her.

"I'm struggling again. The emotional pain is back. I have little energy, and I can't get motivated to do most things," she said, discouraged.

"Sonja is talking about her wish to die." Mitch informed the doctor.

"Have you made any plans to carry out this wish to die?" the doctor asked Sonja.

"Of course not!" Sonja glared at Mitch, clearly upset that he shared this information with the doctor.

"Let's try another antidepressant and see how that goes." The doctor pulled out his prescription pad.

"I don't know if it's related to Sonja's depression, but she also has become obsessed with having everything clean, to the point that she power washed the inside of our car and totaled it," Mitch brought up.

"Wow!" The doctor was stunned. "That sounds like obsessive-compulsive disorder to me. But a trained therapist would be best at diagnosing it. I will give you a referral."

Sonja got a confirmed diagnosis of obsessive-compulsive

disorder, but despite all Mitch's effort to get her treatment, she refused. Sonja didn't feel comfortable talking to a stranger about her problems and didn't want to air her dirty laundry. She also felt therapists were expensive when there was no guarantee that they could help. Therapy felt like such a foreign concept that Sonja fell victim to the many reasons people don't see therapists. Mitch felt stuck with this roadblock.

CHAPTER 14

Bathing

"When was the last time you showered?" Mitch asked Sonja.
"I don't remember, but it's fine." She rolled over in bed.
"Well, I think you're on day ten. So, it's time for a bath." He pulled back the bedcovers.
"No!" She yanked them back on, annoyed.
"Come on." He sat her up.
"I will tomorrow," she bargained.
"Nope." He went into the bathroom and got the tub running.
"Mitch, no. Seriously, not today," she begged.
"Come on." He took her socks off and started undressing her out of clothes she'd been wearing and sleeping in for a week. He guided her to the bathtub, and resentfully she sat in the warm water.
"Are we conditioning or just shampooing your hair today?" he asked.
"Just shampoo," she quietly grumbled.
"Lean back." He poured shampoo on her head and began scrubbing the grease out of her hair. Their eight-year-old son, Alex, walked in and saw Mitch bathing her and quickly went back into their bedroom.
"So, Dad"—Alex peeked in from their bedroom—"is this something I'll need to do for my wife?" he asked seriously.
"I don't know, buddy. Maybe," he told him. *Is it bad that my kids*

know Sonja can't function on her own? he wondered. He had no idea. Mitch worried what his kids' takeaway would be, but he knew this was the only way to keep her afloat.

"Okay, next leg," he instructed Sonja as he shaved her legs. The smell of soap started to wash out her stink. "Lean forward." He scrubbed her back with soap. He wrapped her body in towels and then proceeded to dry her off. She leaned on him as he helped her put on underwear and her black shirt and skirt.

"Mitch, I don't know why this is so hard for me."

He put her back in bed and got her toothbrush and a cup of water.

"Open," he said, hovering the toothbrush by her mouth. He had to brush her teeth for her; otherwise, it wouldn't happen. She took a big sip of water, swished it in her mouth, and spat it back into the cup like it was a portable sink.

"Feel better?" he asked.

"Actually, I do feel a little better," she admitted.

Bathing required a kind of activation energy that she didn't possess, but she was always grateful after it was done.

"I use all the energy I have on the kids, and I'm left with nothing for me, for us. But I love you. You know that, right?" Her eyes searched inside his, and he saw in them the flecks of green that had once made his heart stop. Her eyes remained the window into her soul when he felt she was hard to find. Those green-and-gold flecks were proof that she was the same person he had fallen in love with and didn't feel alive without.

"I know, Sonja." He kissed her forehead.

"Thank you, Mitch." She sighed, lying back down under the covers.

Sonja didn't go from being a fashion maven to sleeping in her clothes and not bathing overnight. It was a slow progression that took years.

It was during their second year of marriage that Sonja slept in her clothes for the first time. She had gotten her first C on a paper and was completely distraught. She cried for hours and curled up in bed, falling asleep completely dressed. But the next day, she woke up and got dressed in another one of her fashionable outfits. Mitch didn't think anything of it or ever suspect this could become her new normal.

After their third year of marriage, sleeping in her clothes became routine. She would tell him she was way too exhausted to get into pajamas, but the next morning, she'd change her clothes, looking fabulous.

By their fifth year of marriage, she had started to not only sleep in her clothes but wear the same outfit, a black cotton T-shirt and skirt, for days at a time. Now her fashionable outfits only showed up on Sundays or special occasions.

As the years went on, bathing only occurred as part of an intervention on Mitch's part. As a child, Mitch was never accused of having patience. He had a quick temper, but Sonja's illness taught him, mostly by sheer force, how to work with what little patience he did have. For years he bathed her, brushed her teeth, and helped her into clean clothes, knowing this was not normal behavior.

He took Sonja to see dozens of doctors during this time. Every one of them diagnosed her with severe depression, which meant Sonja was continually put on many different depression medicines with mixed success. Most doctors recommended therapy, which Mitch was a big supporter of but Sonja continued to outrightly refuse. She believed that if Mitch were only more patient, or if their financial situation would improve, or if she could live in a state she liked, then she'd feel better. There was a strong belief in Sonja that what ailed her was driven by external factors.

Sonja needed Mitch in ways even his children didn't, but he understood the trade-off. If he wanted her to have the energy to raise their children, he needed to give her energy. She was an outstanding mother, always making sure the kids were engaged in life. But her energy deficit was so large he alone could not fill it.

CHAPTER 15

The Feelings Box

"I'm in so much pain!" Sonja screamed. "Being married to you makes me absolutely *miserable*!"

"Stop! You're going to wake up the kids," Mitch tried to whisper.

"It's you! You've made my life hell! I just need to divorce you!" she continued on in a rage. For Sonja, divorce was the threat of choice, and while Mitch definitely did not want one, the threats had become so commonplace, they were hard to take seriously.

"I just think you're in pain. You're not getting better," Mitch said. Sonja was on her sixth antidepressant, and Mitch started to wonder if her diagnosis was right.

"It's our life, your career. You have been working insane hours. And we're barely scraping by, and now we're moving!" She slammed her hands on the counter. "All the decisions you make put me in pain!"

"My decisions? *You* put us in $80,000 debt. That's why we are scraping by and *I've* been working insane hours for years to get those raises, promotions, and bonuses to pay that debt off!" Mitch fought back.

"You decided to leave your job at the hospital to go work with your brother on a startup! That's why we are we moving to Texas!"

"Sonja, you've told me every day for the last *four years* that you don't like Louisiana. I thought moving would be a good thing."

"Yes, but I'm also not ready for a move."

"Well, that would've been great feedback eighteen months ago when I started working with Chris on the business. It would've been really helpful if I'd known you weren't on board," Mitch said in frustration.

"That's because I was fine with it then! But now, I'm not on board." Sonja crossed her arms.

"I can't hit a moving target!" He raised his hands in the air. "Sometimes your behavior can be completely abnormal. You have to see that."

"Maybe I'm perfectly normal and any person would be miserable in this situation!"

"This situation? We are in the top 1 percent of the planet's population. We have a house, food, a wonderful family; we love each other. I'm not getting why our situation equals misery for you!" While Mitch may have been advancing a strong logical argument, he had been losing the emotional argument for years.

"I can't do this *anymore*! I'm just going to kill myself!" She thrashed. Divorce was not the only threat in their conversations; suicidal thoughts being expressed had become commonplace too.

"Sonja, you need therapy."

"No. *You* need therapy!" She pointed at him.

"We *both* need professional help." Mitch didn't know how to handle her suicidal thoughts, and they were scaring him. Sonja just kept telling her doctors she had no plans to take her life so they would let her go home. Frustrated and afraid, Mitch began yelling, "It's been years, and nothing is changing. Do you know what the definition of insanity is? It's doing the same thing over and over again expecting different results. We are living in *insanity*!"

"*Fine!*" she screamed back. "*You* call the therapist, a *marriage* therapist. It's the only therapist I'm willing to see!"

―――

The marriage therapist pulled his hands into a ball around his chest, pretending to hide a box. "All of us have a tender and vulnerable feelings box inside of us." He opened his skinny fingers as he looked at Sonja and Mitch. "Inside this box are the emotions we don't want to reveal. I'm ashamed. I'm jealous. I'm insecure. I don't feel valued." The therapist relaxed in his seat and looked at Sonja. "What are the vulnerable feelings you're experiencing right now?" he asked, tipping his gaze over his glasses.

"I feel weak." Sonja started crying.

"And Mitch?" The therapist tilted his head.

Mitch took a breath and turned to Sonja. "I feel sad and empty." He paused. "I feel like you need me but you don't care for me."

"Are you kidding me?" she instantly scoffed.

"I know you value the kids. They're your everything. But when it comes to me, I feel more like a means to an end—someone you need things from—but you don't think I need anything in return," he said honestly.

"You think I don't care about you? *Seriously!*" Sonja became explosive. "I love you; why do you think I'm still here?" She stomped her foot. "It will never be enough!" She slapped her hands on her legs. "I can't take having another thing to work on! So just don't even go there." Her anger melted into violent tears.

"Sonja, maybe I should work with you one on one." The therapist gave Mitch a concerned look as she sobbed.

"What? No. This is an *us* problem, not a *me* problem." She wiped her tears.

"That may be, but we won't be able to get to the 'us' problems until we address the 'you' problems," the therapist advised.

"I think we're done here." Sonja suddenly composed herself. "Mitch, let's go."

Sonja already had a thousand knives in her, and bringing up more pain points was just another knife she didn't have the room to fit. They tried many marriage therapists, each time with the same result—the therapist recommended they work with Sonja alone before doing any marriage therapy.

One therapist forcefully told Sonja her big emotions were the underlying issue in their marriage. That was the last time Sonja agreed to therapy. She fought against the indication she was the broken one, and so Mitch was left to deal with their issues on his own.

Marriage therapists frequently say that when couples have difficulties, "it takes two to tango." But when a severe mental illness is involved, it really only takes one—the illness. You can think you're fighting with each other, when in reality you're both just fighting the illness.

Yet not one therapist or doctor had given Sonja a diagnosis other than depression and OCD. Maybe it was because they moved around so much that they kept starting at square one with each new doctor. Or that mental health was a topic that was not openly discussed or understood during that time. The stigmas surrounding mental health keep many people quiet, confused, and undiagnosed, and Mitch and Sonja belonged to that group.

CHAPTER 16

Dinner Party

Sugarland, Texas
2002

Mitch and his brother's startup was struggling to raise money. The 9/11 terrorist attacks had caused several of their financial backers to withdraw investment commitments due to the global uncertainty. The company was generating $2 million a year in sales, but without more outside funding, it would be difficult to grow the business. Mitch drove home from work worrying that moving to Texas for this company had been riskier than he had realized. Sonja didn't want him to try a startup, and he worried she might have been right.

Once parked in the garage, he sat in the car and gripped the torn steering wheel. He closed his eyes and took a deep breath. He could no longer share his difficulties with Sonja without creating more chaos. She couldn't handle the appearance of bad news and was emotionally unstable even when things were going well. Carrying hardships on your own is a whole different type of lonely. It's not the lonely where you have a free weekend but no friends to call, or the lonely that makes you notice all the couples around you while you eat alone. Mitch had a wife, he had kids, he had his unit, yet he had to hide away a large portion of his worries and his life from the very person he needed to tell most—his wife. He had never been a person who needed to vent, but he and Sonja had told each other the details of each other's lives for so long that slowly losing his ability to share things with her felt like losing a piece of his best friend.

Sonja and Mitch were having guests over for dinner, and Mitch would fake his way through the evening just like he did at work, church, or any other social function. He was losing himself, forgetting who he really was, caught up in playing a fictious character, like he had done in high school theater.

Mitch's family came from Britain. The family culture was to keep a stiff upper lip in adversity, remain resolute and unemotional when faced with trials. He grabbed his briefcase and walked inside the house like the good soldier his parents had taught him to be.

"Should I put the vase here, or does it overcrowd the table?" Sonja set her flower arrangement in the center of the table, looking at Mitch standing in the doorway.

"It might be hard to see the person across from you," Mitch said.

"That's what I thought." She snapped her fingers.

She plucked the arrangement off the table and moved it to the kitchen island. She had draped tablecloths over the scratched furniture, and what they lacked in space in their tiny home she made up for in fresh flowers. Pots of pasta boiled on the stove as she kept nervously checking the time and the clouds of steam made the kitchen feel humid.

"They should be here any minute." She enthusiastically stirred the pasta sauce. Sonja's moods had become even bigger and more inconsistent over the months. It was surreal to watch her one moment be sobbing and shaking in a corner of the house and then be completely composed while talking to her sister on the phone without a care in the world. Her daily behavior continually perplexed Mitch, leaving him utterly confused.

Just then the doorbell rang. "Mitch, keep stirring!" She excitedly kissed him as she handed him the spoon and went to open the door.

"Hi, Sonja!" he heard Amy say.

Once the entire dinner party of six couples had arrived, they split the guests up between the kitchen and dining room because neither room was big enough to fit everyone.

"How cute is this!" The women swooned over Sonja's dinner table display.

Most of these people lived in multimillion-dollar homes; many were investors in Mitch and Chris's medical device company. Sonja wasn't embarrassed to entertain them in her $120,000 home because she didn't equate money or belongings with a person's worth. This was one of Mitch's favorite qualities in Sonja.

"Okay, so I'm not a cook, but I think my spaghetti turned out good." Sonja tapped the wooden sauce spoon on the side of the metal pot.

Amy pulled a chair out to sit down but hit the back of the chair into the wall, making a loud bang. "Oops, I'm so sorry." She looked up, embarrassed.

"Don't worry. I do it all the time. It's not your fault," Mitch piped in.

"Oh, let me get you guys ice." Sonja threw her hands up, rushing to take her guests' cups.

"I love the wallpaper in your guest bathroom," one of the women complimented her.

"Oh, thank you. I thought the red added a nice pop," Sonja beamed, scooping ice into cups.

Distantly, Mitch watched Sonja. There was an undeniable presence and force that radiated from her very being. A single look from her was so compelling that it drew people to her. Yet, her pain caused her to build a fortress so tall that she didn't have close friends, only associates.

After the dinner guests had left, Sonja turned on some music while she and Mitch cleaned up. Mitch stood at the sink drying dishes when Sonja came up and hugged him from behind.

"Tonight was fun, wasn't it?" She smiled on his neck.

"You were a great host." Mitch turned around and kissed her.

At times like this, Mitch wanted to hold Sonja so tight that she couldn't slip away. But no matter what he did to keep her, she always disappeared to some unknown place.

CHAPTER 17

Secrets in Plain Sight

As Mitch walked into their bedroom closet to grab a T-shirt to sleep in, he noticed a white powder dusted all over his shirt. He patted his hand behind the stacks of folded clothes when his hand landed in a pile of donuts.

"Ugh, she's hiding food again." He sighed, gathering up the powdered donuts. Pushing the clothes to the side, he saw mounds of candy bars and boxes of cookies. Sonja had hoarding tendencies in the way she shopped for clothes and the way she shopped for food. She bought in bulk, and she stashed it all away in their closet for safekeeping.

Before getting into bed, Mitch brushed all the cookie crumbs off the sheets. While living in Texas, Sonja had gained over a hundred pounds. Food had become one of her pain relievers. She would eat until she felt sick and lie in bed reading romance novels until she felt well enough to get up and eat again.

"Does me being fat bother you?" Sonja asked.

"I don't care if I have an overweight wife. I care if I have a happy wife," Mitch said.

"Well, do you think I'm happy?"

He needed to answer that question carefully to avoid a toxic fight he didn't have the energy to see through. She looked at him, waiting for an answer.

"I think you're in pain and you're coping through food," he answered.

"Food does make me feel better," she admitted.

"I know but being overweight is one thing; abusing your body is something completely different. Your family needs a healthy mom." He worried that soon Sonja wouldn't only be dealing with emotional issues but with physical ones as well.

"I've tried dozens of weight-loss programs, and none of them have worked. I just keep gaining weight."

"You need to focus on taking care of yourself," he said, wondering if it was even possible.

Mitch was surprised when Sonja got a job at a hospital being a phlebotomist. She had done phlebotomy while they were in graduate school out of necessity, and it had caused her a lot of distress. So, he couldn't figure out why she was doing that type of work again.

"What are you doing?" Mitch blinked. The kids held ankle weights up to Sonja's body as she duct-taped them in place.

"Hold it right there, Lincoln." Sonja bit off a strip of duct tape as their five-year-old son struggled to hold the weight in place on her thigh.

"Mom is going to a doctor's appointment, and they are going to weigh her," Rachael told him.

"She doesn't weigh enough," Alex chimed in.

"What doctor's appointment?" Mitch asked.

"I'm going to get gastric bypass surgery, and I need to make sure I qualify."

"Sonja, don't do that; it seems dishonest," he said, shocked that she thought this was necessary. "And there's no way they won't notice."

"Mitchell, just stop. This is a formality," she snapped. "It's not like I'm not gonna get heavier on my own. Without this surgery, my weight will keep climbing."

"And how are you going to pay for the surgery?"

"That's why I got the job at the hospital. Their insurance covers it." She smiled, pleased with herself.

"Well, don't make the kids a part of it."

"Do you *really* want to fight about this right now?" She dropped her skirt, ready to go to war, covered in weights and all.

He looked at the kids and let it go. She was such a force of nature. There were many times he had to choose to either go to war and destroy the household in the process or let her be. He decided that in this case, fighting with her was a waste of breath.

Sonja did qualify and got the surgery. For the first time in years, she started losing weight, and she stopped binge eating. Mitch was excited that Sonja was making progress in her health and overall well-being. This gave him hope that she had the ability to make the changes necessary to have a healthy life. But Mitch also knew Sonja would do what Sonja thought was best, even if Mitch disagreed or thought it was irrational. That realization was driven home when his brother Chris pulled him aside at work.

"Um, Mitch, Ken was biking to the office this morning and said he saw Sonja outside doing yard work"—he paused—"in her underwear."

"What?" Mitch stood aghast.

"Yes, Mitch. Gardening in her underwear!"

Mitch had no words; even for Sonja this seemed extreme. Ken was not only a coworker of his but also the bishop of their local church congregation.

"You should really talk to her about that," Chris advised.

"I have no more control over Sonja than a complete stranger," he admitted. And that was the truth.

People could look at a lot of individual circumstances in their marriage and say, "Oh, Mitch is being too passive," or "He backs down too quickly," but really, he was making a never-ending string of active choices. He had to make judgment calls on what he thought was *most important* for their family, and rarely did those things include fighting with Sonja to stop gardening in her underwear or duct-taping weights on her body for her weigh-in. When it came to Sonja, Mitch became good at controlling flames—letting small fires burn and putting larger ones out.

CHAPTER 18

David

Mitch watched Sonja talk to her sister over the phone as she paced back and forth. "How did this happen?" Sonja panicked, gripping the phone. She covered her mouth with her hand and started crying.

"What's wrong?" he whispered.

She cried harder.

"Sonja, what's wrong?" Mitch started to panic too.

"He tried to asphyxiate himself in a truck," she snapped.

"Who?"

"My dad tried to kill himself, Mitchell." She shook her head.

"What! Is he all right?"

"Luckily, my brother and sister found him in time."

"Is he okay?" Mitch hugged her.

"He was put in the psych ward today, and they diagnosed him with bipolar disorder."

"Really?" he said, taken aback.

Mitch didn't know much about bipolar disorder, but as David was in his sixties, it seemed like a strange time to be diagnosed, after all those years. He was largely full of energy, and Mitch couldn't think of many times when he saw him depressed. Mitch knew the stress of his legal battles often caused him to go into a downward spiral, but this was the severest low he had seen.

Sonja and Mitch flew out to visit her dad in the psych ward.

"We're here to see David Nemelka," Mitch said to the front desk attendant.

"Oh, we *all* know David Nemelka." The receptionist looked up. "He'll be in the break room." She pointed down the hall. Mitch held Sonja's hand and tried to comfort her as they walked in to visit her dad.

"Sonja! Mitch!" David excitedly threw his hands up. He sat in the center of five other patients. "Can we put this on pause?" He looked around the group. "Come on over! Meet my friends!" David waved them over.

Mitch and Sonja had gone to the psych ward to visit David with the expectation that it would be a somber visit; clearly, they were wrong.

"This is Jared, Clair, Pippin, Hon, and Sam." He pointed them out.

"Hi." They smiled.

"And this is my daughter Sonja and her husband, Mitch." He shook Mitch's shoulders.

"David, we need more dice." A short, skinny man approached him. "We don't have enough for all the players."

"What great news; the games are a hit!" David loudly clapped his hands. "Have some happiness gum." David pulled a pack of Juicy Fruit out of a Walmart bag he had been carrying around.

"But we need more dice." The man fidgeted.

"Don't worry, Pippin. I'll have Ingrid bring more dice tomorrow," he promised.

"How fun; they hold game nights?" Sonja asked, looking around the common room at all the board game stations that had been set up.

"Oh no, this is just a little something I set up for the patients," he whispered, momentarily forgetting he was a patient himself.

"So, how are you?" Sonja asked her dad seriously.

"Ready to go home." He looked at her. "Doctor Hales!" he yelled down the hall. "Catch!" He threw a pack of gum toward him.

"Thanks!" The doctor laughed.

This did not look like a person who wanted to die. He looked like a popular kid at a summer camp. Mitch didn't know how he acted around other family members, but perhaps he had some depressive days in between all the energetic ones. Mitch stood there in shock as David passed out happiness gum to *everyone*—patients, nurses, and doctors.

"I'll be right back." David left and joined a patient at a table. They talked for a while as Sonja and Mitch awkwardly stood in the psych ward.

"What a strange place," Sonja whispered to Mitch as she continued to look around.

Mitch too thought it was a strange place, this small, run-down facility that housed big personalities like David.

"David!" one of the nurses shouted, cantering over to him.

"When you get home, you can stop your medicine if it's too much. Keep your chin up," David loudly whispered to a patient, patting them on the shoulder.

"David! No!" She shook her finger at him. "You aren't licensed. You can't advise them on medication!"

"Whoa, whoa, whoa." David put his hands up innocently. "I'm not here to undermine authority. Just sharing hope where I can."

"You have got to stop giving therapy sessions to the patients. Some of our patients are listening to you over our doctors," she huffed.

David lived very little (if any) of his life within the rules and boundaries society put up. So, it was no surprise the psych ward was no different. He couldn't just be a patient. A typical patient might make a friend or two and then leave with some meds. But not David Nemelka. In addition to being the favorite friend and gamer of the whole facility, he had now added "therapist" to his life résumé. He held one-on-one meetings with other patients while he himself was a patient. He blurred lines and confidently did what he felt was best to aid people struggling, and honestly that was part of what made him so lovable.

Sonja's dad helped many people but had a blind spot when it came to himself. Sonja and Mitch had been on the receiving end of his kindness numerous times, but now he needed help. Real help. But he seemed to ignore that fact.

David got released from the hospital with his medication. He couldn't stand taking it because of how effectively it took his mania away. He loved his mania, and a large portion of his identity was wrapped up with being manic. It gave him enormous amounts of energy and made life thrilling, despite the collateral damage it created. David simply didn't know who he was without it, and so he fought the medication.

Even though several doctors evaluated Sonja for bipolar disorder and her diagnosis continued to come back as extreme depression and OCD, Mitch had his doubts. Despite what the testing said, he wondered if Sonja had the same illness as her father. He did know that the antidepressants and therapy they had done hadn't been able to touch what Sonja was going through. As Mitch continued to lose his wife to some undiagnosed force, he began to believe stronger and stronger that undiagnosed force was bipolar disorder.

CHAPTER 19

The Fight Pattern

Sonja and Mitch had gotten into a predictable pattern of having the morning fight before he went to work, the afternoon fight when she called him at work, and the evening fight right before bed. If they were awake, there was tension. He just wanted a truce where they could agree to let everything go and have what they had in their first couple years of marriage, when they didn't fight at all. But it wasn't so simple.

Time was supposed to heal all wounds, but for Sonja, time just gathered more wounds. There was an overwhelming accumulation of past pain and arguments that would resurface in every fight. Apologies, compromises, concessions, and empathetic listening didn't seem to work down the pile of past offenses and emotional pain. Sonja's unbearable pain seemed to scream its way through their marriage. Mitch felt he was in such a deficit that even if he achieved perfection as a husband, the prior years of suffering would still be fair game for arguments.

"I just want to die! I'm gonna kill myself. I'm gonna find a way!" Sonja threw a book at the wall. "I did research on the internet today on how to make sure I end up dead," she informed him.

Her thoughts about death and killing herself had frighteningly become a daily conversation. Although in his heart he couldn't believe that his wife would actually go through with it, he still was worried enough that he had taken Sonja to the ER and shared his concern with the doctor. But Sonja was convincing enough during the visit that she would never attempt suicide that the doctor agreed with her and advised against hospitalization. Yet Mitch knew there was something serious affecting her, and he needed to help her understand that as well.

"Sonja, I think you need to be open to the possibility that a lot of your unhappiness isn't just about your external situation. Have you considered that you might be bipolar?" he cautiously asked. "Your dad was diagnosed as bipolar."

"I've been tested! I don't have it! I'm just stressed!" she screamed.

"Also, some of your cousins are bipolar, as is your aunt," he carefully proceeded.

"One of my cousins had a vision that he needed to convert Tiger Woods to Christianity. I haven't had any visions. And my other cousin is in jail for counterfeiting and faking his death. You think I'm a criminal?" She dug in her heels.

"I never said you are a criminal or delusional, Sonja. But you're suicidal."

"Everyone wants to die, Mitchell. I personally know six people who have died from suicide. It's common."

"Actually, it's not; most people want to live. I think this is way bigger than you being depressed or having a bad marriage. I think you have a severe mental illness."

"Oh, great, so now it's me! I'm just crazy, and it has nothing to do with you. I *refuse* to belong to a group of people deemed crazy and violent." Sonja remained hardened to the idea.

The stigmas around mental illness were so powerful that they had stopped Sonja from being completely open and honest with herself and her doctors.

"Sonja this has nothing to do with you being crazy or violent. You are sick. That I do know."

"I hate you! I'm going to divorce you!"

Mitch grabbed her shoulders and searched into her eyes. "I love you, Sonja. I have always loved you." He pulled her into his arms. "I know this isn't you talking. Please, Sonja, please just listen."

"I can't love someone who thinks I'm mentally ill!" She forcefully shoved him away. "I can't keep living like this!" she screamed at the top of her lungs and threw another book at the wall that ended up hitting him in the head.

"Ouch!" He grabbed his head and felt a large, pulsing welt forming.

Sonja began crying in earnest as she stormed out of the room.

Mitch pulled his hand away and saw blood in his palm. He grabbed a towel and pressed it on the side of his head. With his back against the wall, he slid down to the floor, completely defeated.

God, if you want this to work, we need help now! Mitch prayed fervently. It was a prayer he had offered up hundreds of times, and each time, the next day might be 10 percent better. Not fixed, but just enough to bear it another day.

For Mitch, simply surviving gave rise to a sliver of hope that maybe one day Sonja would be better. Hope is a funny thing. It's what dragged him through one day to the next, then through weeks that became months, and months that became years, until he was in so deep, he realized he had to keep going because the end had to be closer than a new beginning.

CHAPTER 20

A New Normal

Baton Rouge, Louisiana
2006

As life does, it blazed by without a pause for Mitch to catch his breath. The medical device startup company had been sold to a publicly traded company, which helped him pay off the rest of their debt. Then Ochsner called and asked if he wanted to come back and work for them in Baton Rouge, Louisiana, where they needed help with an underperforming hospital. Mitch was excited about the challenge and grateful for the pay increase it would offer. Even though he had paid off the debt through hard work, he still carried the scar of money insecurity.

They had enrolled the kids in a public magnet school, thinking it would be better than the public schools, which were pretty rough in Baton Rouge, Louisiana.

"Do you think we took a wrong turn?" Sonja said, hopeful.

"No, that's the school right there." Mitch pointed to the run-down school, shocked.

"Mitch, the school is right next to all those boarded-up houses. Look, people are sitting on their porches, smoking weed. They look like they are selling drugs too. Did you see that exchange?"

"Yep. Exchanging money probably for marijuana." Mitch turned the car around. "Our kids are *not* going to that school."

"Where are we going to school then?" Alex asked, staring out the car window at all the people smoking weed.

"Can't we go back to our schools in Albuquerque?" Lincoln begged.

"Kids, we will figure this out," Sonja said, determined.

They pulled up to Rachael's school, which was brand new.

"This looks like a nice school," Rachael said, hopeful.

"I'll walk you in. Everyone, wait in the car," Mitch said.

Mitch and Rachael walked in, and the first thing they witnessed was a kid pushed against his locker, getting handcuffed. There were armed guards patrolling the hallways.

"Let's get out of here." Mitch grabbed Rachael's hand.

They decided to homeschool their children. Mitch and Sonja hired math and English teachers to teach their kids. Sonja taught history and science. Mitch had the kids on a waiting list for private school, but each year, Sonja refused to enroll them.

Alex and Lincoln wanted to be professional tennis players, and Sonja took their dream seriously. She obsessively researched how many hours kids needed to practice to go pro and built a homeschooling schedule around those hours. They had a private tennis coach and practiced five to six hours a day, six days a week. Sonja felt putting in this type of work was only worth it if the boys went pro. Mitch disagreed. He didn't care whether or not his sons ever became professional tennis players; he saw the hard work as its own end.

After a year in Baton Rouge, Sonja began having trouble sleeping at night. For Mitch, it felt like having a newborn again, but her illness was much more demanding than a newborn's, which couldn't be quieted by a feeding or changing. He'd often would go to work on two to three hours of sleep and rely on energy drinks to get him through the day.

On one of those nights, Mitch awoke to the sound of Sonja crying in another room. "Sonja?" He threw the blanket off him and went to search for her. He walked into the kitchen, the lights blinding his tired eyes. She was sitting on the stone-cold floor, in a corner, huddled and shaking. He sat down next to her, lifted her onto his lap, and tucked her safely into his arms. She snuggled in as close as she could, sobbing. It broke his heart to see her awakened by the same emotional pain that disturbed her throughout the day. Even in sleep she couldn't escape it.

"Do you need me to make you some herbal tea?" he asked as he gently stroked her hair.

"Yes," she moaned. As the water heated up in the microwave, Mitch continued to stroke her hair as she pressed her face into his chest. "The pain keeps waking me up," she cried.

"I know. I'm sorry." Mitch rubbed her back. The microwave beeped, and he stirred honey and almond milk into the steaming cup. Mitch waited as she sipped her tea. "Cutie, let's get you back to bed."

They climbed back into bed, and Mitch drew Sonja in close to him as he looked at the clock. It was 1:00 a.m., and he had to get up in four hours for work.

"I can't sleep." Sonja wiped a tear.

"Let me get you a sleeping pill," he offered.

"I've already taken two." They never did seem to help.

"Okay, I'll draw a bath, and then we can watch a Barbie princess movie. Do you want *12 Dancing Princesses* or *The Princess and the Pauper*?"

"*12 Dancing Princesses.*"

Happy movies where the villain was not too scary and the story was simple and childlike had a soothing effect on Sonja.

She paced the bathroom, still periodically bursting into sobs, as he drew the bath. Once the tub was high enough, she slid into the hot water. He added more lavender salts to the water, and her crying tapered down to a whimpering. By the time she was dried off and the movie was playing, she had calmed down.

Mitch lay in bed next to her, watching Sonja's emotions rise and fall with Barbie's. Whenever Barbie and her love interest talked to each other, Sonja got a small, unconscious grin on her face, despite the watery tears still in her eyes. He still found her so lovable, even in the middle of their emotional storm. He put his wax earplugs in and turned away from the TV light, trying to get in what little sleep he could.

Only an hour later, he was again awakened by Sonja's intense crying. The bathroom door was cracked open, and the light spilled into the bedroom. He took his earplugs out and quickly got up. *Oh no*, he thought to himself as he hurriedly pushed the door open.

"Sonja?" Mitch saw her sitting on the floor, curled up tight, holding a knife with blood pooled at her feet.

He slowly approached her. "Give me the knife," he calmly said.

"I need it. It's the only thing that numbs the pain." She cradled the knife to her chest. He didn't want to spook her and have her run away or lock herself in a closet.

"Sonja," he steadily said as he slowly knelt at eye level with her. Mitch put his hand on hers and carefully lifted each finger off the knife's handle until it was free. Sonja dropped her head on her knees. "Let's get you cleaned up." He put Neosporin on her cuts and taped Band-Aids over them. She limped her way back to the bed, and he tucked her in.

"I'm sorry," she cried.

"I know." He stroked her hair.

"But you have to understand it helps me. It releases the tension associated with my emotional pain."

He honestly did not know how to handle this new behavior. So, he said nothing as he continued to stroke her as she cried herself back to sleep.

A short time later, his alarm went off, and he reluctantly went back in the bathroom to get ready for work. He saw the steak knife and put it in the kitchen sink like someone clearing the dinner table.

How did self-harm become a part of our life? Mitch thought. Had he been too dismissive of her symptoms? Could he have prevented this if he had forced her to get individual therapy? He had his fair share of fights with Sonja, but he never forced her to do anything. Was that the problem here? Was he relying too heavily on her to make choices that would help her get better?

He wondered if he was going crazy along with Sonja. She was getting sicker and sicker, and he was becoming more accustomed to it, like it was normal. They had seen doctors and therapists, tried dozens of medications, made trips to the ER, and Mitch was left feeling like he had failed her. It didn't matter if he believed Sonja was bipolar; if he couldn't get a professional to agree and break the news to her, nothing would change.

The only option he had left was to admit her to a psychiatric hospital, the same place her dad finally got diagnosed. He knew Sonja would never go willingly, so he decided to try a new approach to getting her well, sheer force. And he would need reinforcements.

CHAPTER 21

Reinforcements

Baton Rouge, Louisiana
2007

"Hey, Mitch!" David's cheerful, booming voice came through on the other end of the phone. "How are you? How's the family?" he happily asked.

Mitch, being an intensely private person, had never given her family the full extent of his and Sonja's situation. "Things aren't good. It's about Sonja. She's threatening to kill herself, throwing things, crying until she's so tired she falls asleep, and now she's started self-harming. I'm not sure how long this has been going on, but from the looks of her feet, last night wasn't the first night. I'm going to hospitalize her, and I need your help because she's not going to go willingly," Mitch pleaded.

David had been out of the hospital for some time and was experiencing a period of stability, which was fortunate, given that Mitch felt David was to be a critical piece in his plan to hospitalize Sonja.

David let out a thoughtful sigh. "We have been concerned about her for a long time."

"If I admit her to the psych ward, I think there's a real possibility she'll divorce me." Mitch didn't want to get divorced. He had been fiercely fighting for their marriage.

David busted up laughing. "Divorce you? No, she needs you! She loves you, Mitch. She's not going anywhere."

Mitch hoped that was true but wasn't as confident as David. He believed that she would really divorce him or that if they stayed married, her involuntary hospitalization would be cannon fodder in every fight for years to come. There was nothing he wanted more than to get out of this hell still married and with his family intact.

Sonja's parents flew into the Baton Rouge airport and went straight to the ER, where David told the hospital's Community Outreach for Psychiatric Emergencies (COPE) team that later in the day, Mitch would be admitting his suicidal daughter to the psych ward against her will. He gave them a rundown of her medical history and prepared them for the fact that she'd be a fighter.

"Kids, come downstairs! Omi and Opa's rental car just pulled up!" Sonja yelled to the kids.

Mitch was so nervous that sweat beaded down his back as Sonja's parents pulled into the driveway. She thought her parents were making a friendly, impromptu visit to see the boys' tennis match that day and was unaware of the real reason for their trip.

"Be careful not to bend the corner," Rachael whispered to Alex.

Mitch watched as Rachael, Alex, and Lincoln carried down a homemade welcome sign they had made from twelve sheets of printer paper held together with Scotch tape and decorated with Magic Markers.

"That turned out great!" Mitch forced a smile.

"They're here!" Sonja yelled with excitement.

She adored her family, which is what made the secret behind this trip so hard. The back door opened, and there stood Sonja's mom and dad. Mitch's eyes locked with Sonja's dad's, and he gave him an encouraging smile before shifting his attention to the kids.

"Now, where are the three people I flew all this way to see?" David shouted, tucking his hands behind his suspenders.

"Opa!" The kids ran into his arms.

Later that day, everyone sat watching Alex's and Lincoln's tennis matches under shaded benches. Aside from hearing the occasional grunt and pop of a tennis ball on a racket, Mitch couldn't concentrate on anything but what would happen next.

"We're going to head back to your house. I'm tired," Sonja's mom said halfway through the boys' match.

"Okay. We'll meet you back at the house when they're done," Sonja said, eyes locked on the courts.

"Sonja, you should come with us," her dad said.

"No, I want to stay and watch the match." Her eyes followed the ball as it flew across the net.

"Sonja, you need to come with us," her dad said firmly. She glanced at him, a bit surprised, and then turned her head back to the court.

"I don't want to come."

"Sonja, please come with us," he practically begged.

"You don't see your parents often. Go with them," Mitch said, trying to convince her without giving any hint that this was a setup.

"All right, all right, I'll go." She put her hands up in defeat. "I'll see you at home." She quickly kissed Mitch goodbye.

He grabbed her hand and pulled her in tight for another kiss, wondering if that would be the last kiss he'd ever get from her. In a matter of hours, Sonja would know the real reason her parents came, and Mitch worried she may never forgive him for what he was about to do.

"I love you, Sonja," he whispered as he watched her walk away in her naivete alongside her dad and knew there was no turning back now. She was about to hate him, possibly forever, but he knew this is what she needed. Part of him wanted to run to her and call the whole thing off before the bomb undoubtedly went off, but he loved her too much—he had to save her, even if that meant losing her.

The plan was for David and Ingrid to get Sonja alone in the car and share with her their concern about her mental health and invite her to go to the psychiatric hospital voluntarily. But if that didn't work, they'd have to resort to plan B, and Mitch would need to hospitalize her involuntarily.

After the match, Mitch drove the kids home, and Sonja was standing in the carport, fuming with her arms crossed. He got out of the car, and her eyes were piercing into his. *Plan B it is*, Mitch thought to himself. Sonja's dad stood at her side, trying to talk her down.

Mitch turned to the kids. "Go upstairs and find Omi. Maybe you could play a game with her." As the kids piled out of the car, David waved them upstairs.

"You've gathered notes on me? Is this some sort of blackmail?" Sonja furiously whispered to Mitch.

"Sonja, let's sit down and talk about this." Mitch corralled her inside.

"Are you all crazy?" She desperately looked at her dad and then Mitch.

"You're going to the hospital," her dad firmly stated.

"No. I'm not!" She picked up a kitchen chair and threw it against the wood floor. "I'm not going!" Another chair flew from her hands. "I'm not!" she screamed amid the sound of the second chair hitting the floor.

These tantrums had become commonplace over the years, but the context of this situation intensified her rage, and Mitch's heart started racing. Mitch noticed his kids had not gone upstairs but quietly stood in the corner, watching the scene play out. He quickly grabbed his kids' hands and took them upstairs to the playroom, trying to protect them from the situation. Sonja's mom was quietly knitting in a chair, trying to stay out of the line of fire.

Mitch gathered all three of his children in his arms. "It's going to be okay." He tried reassuring them, but the words felt hollow. How could a thirteen-, eleven-, and eight-year-old even begin to process what was happening around them? Mitch had told himself thousands of times that Sonja's and his love for their kids would be enough. That love heals all wounds. Yet in his most quiet moments, the harsh reality would creep in that he didn't know what impact Sonja's illness would have on his children's lives. Would they need years of therapy, maybe even a lifetime? And would their childhood trauma haunt them into future relationships? Mitch readily admitted he had told himself a story about their lives that he could live with instead of acknowledging many painful truths that felt unbearable.

Sonja thundered into the room with David behind her. The kids scurried away from Mitch, knowing Sonja would be coming straight for him.

She stood in front of Mitch, pointing a stiff finger at him. "If you hospitalize me, I will divorce you. It will be over!" The intensity of her threat made it the most convincing one to date.

He didn't flinch. They stood, eyes locked, resolute in their conviction of how this war should end.

"That's a chance I'm willing to take," Mitch replied firmly.

He braced himself for what she would do next, but she just stood there staring at him. Mitch held his ground and stared back into her eyes, seeing the torment that never seemed to leave her.

The kids stood courageously next to Omi. Rachael protectively held each one of her brothers' hands, focused. Her eyes darted back and forth between her parents. Mitch glanced over at his little brave soldiers, so composed, not one of them shedding a single tear. He knew his kids didn't have the luxury to express the emotions children commonly exhibited. Sonja's enormous emotions left little room for anyone else to freely let their feelings flow out.

"You did this. You're the reason my family's falling apart!" Sonja frantically turned to her dad.

"Would you just go to the emergency room and talk with a doctor?" her dad lovingly asked. "Tell them everything, and if they say you can come home, then that will be good enough for us," he said with his hand on his heart.

Sonja's eyes drifted to her kids. They cautiously met her gaze, unsure what her next move would be. Mitch watched as tears started to roll down Sonja's cheeks. He never doubted her devotion to their children, but that wasn't enough to shield them from the wreckage of her emotional storms. They got injured every time.

"You promise if the doctor says I can go home, all this talk about the hospital will stop?" she asked, her eyes never leaving her children's faces.

"I promise." Her dad gathered Sonja in his arms for one of his bear hugs.

"Why don't you pack a bag, just in case?" her mom added.

Sonja left the room without another word.

Mitch immediately looked at his children. He held out a hand to them, signaling that it was safe to come over. The current storm had calmed for the moment. Rachael led her brothers to their dad, still tightly holding their hands.

"If you get divorced, I'll live with Mom. Don't worry, I'll take care of her," Rachael said, determined to be a part of the solution.

"Well, I'm going with Dad," Alex said without a moment's hesitation.

Lincoln said nothing, but his eyes revealed he was unsure what to do next.

Mitch took all their little hands and put his over them. "No matter what, we will always be a family. Nothing will sever us."

Sonja walked into the room dressed in a black skirt, flowing white blouse, and black high heels with glittering diamond bracelets hanging on her wrists. She was holding an overnight bag that looked empty.

"Sonja, you look pretty," her mom commented.

"What game are you playing?" David quickly asked.

"I have a church meeting later tonight," she said, raising her chin up.

"You're going to the ER right now. That was the deal," David said sharply.

"I know," Sonja said, unintimidated.

"You might get admitted," her dad said, trying to clear up any confusion.

Sonja held up her overnight bag.

Lincoln broke free from his troop and ran to Sonja. "Mom!" he wailed, frantically wrapping his arms around her waist. "Don't go!"

"She needs to go, Lincoln," Rachael firmly said. Full of fortitude, she walked over and hugged Sonja the way a mother would an upset child. "Don't worry, Mom. I know you're scared, but everything is going to be just fine."

Alex stayed by Mitch, watching his siblings say goodbye to Sonja. He stood stoically, not moving an inch. Mitch was his boat in their family's stormy sea. He relied on Mitch more heavily than any of the other children. Alex was an extremely serious child, and Mitch didn't know if he was born that way or his environment had made him that way.

Sonja looked over at Alex and walked over to him. She gently took his face in her hands and quietly said, "My little man," an endearment she and Mitch called Alex. Alex didn't move or make a single facial expression. He just gazed into his mother's eyes, emotionless.

Mitch put his arm around Alex. "It's going to be okay, buddy." Alex looked up at Mitch and stepped closer to him.

Sonja interrupted, "Let's get this over with." She forcefully brushed past Mitch toward the car.

"Kids, we are all going to be okay," Mitch reassured them as he kissed each of their heads and followed Sonja out.

CHAPTER 22

The Emergency Room

Sonja sat fidgeting on the exam table, and Mitch sat in a chair in the corner, watching her in silence. She avoided eye contact with him but whispered, "I've called my sister Allyson and my brother Mike, and they're both attorneys, and they said I could have *you* admitted to the hospital. Maybe you're crazy!"

"Okay." He sighed, knowing full well she hadn't called anyone.

"Let me write up notes about you and show them to a doctor! Then you'd be sitting where I am right now," she fumed.

A nurse came in. "They're ready to see you." She led them through light-gray hallways until they entered a room with four chairs and a small coffee table, where a COPE evaluator would assess Sonja.

A woman entered the room. "Hi, Mrs. Wasden. I'm a crisis worker. I'm here to evaluate you." She extended her hand.

"But I'm not in crisis." Sonja dodged the handshake.

"Then what brings you to the emergency room?" she asked.

"Just stress." Sonja began ticking off each stressful event with her fingers. "I've moved, been living in a house that's being renovated, recently lost a hundred pounds, and I'm homeschooling my three children."

Mitch knew Sonja's issues were so much more than homeschooling and tennis stress. The problem was he could never get Sonja to see that, and no doctor could give them a firm diagnosis, which left them in perpetual limbo. He had to believe this time would be different.

"Have you ever thought about suicide?" the woman inquired, getting down to business. Mitch wondered if Sonja would answer honestly.

"Who hasn't?" she said. Sonja had deluded herself into thinking every person wanted to die and that suicidal thoughts, feelings, and urges were not just common but in fact normal.

"In what ways have you thought about suicide?" the woman continued.

Mitch closed his eyes and braced himself. He didn't want to hear all the ways his wife fantasized about ending her life.

"Jumping off a building, driving my car into an oncoming semi-truck, standing in front of a semitruck and have it run me over—" That was her favorite. "Taking pills, drowning myself, or stabbing myself and bleeding to death." She paused. "But no guns. That's where I draw the line."

The type of pain a person had to be in to contemplate these things still blew his mind, and no matter what he did to try to protect his wife from this type of pain, it never worked. Mitch reached over and took her hand in his. Sonja didn't seem to notice.

"Have you ever attempted suicide?" Sonja shook her head. "And why haven't you tried any of those things?"

"I don't think I could face God if I did," Sonja answered openly.

"Do you want to die?" she asked calmly.

He wanted to stop the words from coming out of her mouth, but they came out anyway.

"Yes," Sonja said with such conviction that it caused Mitch to flinch. "Can I go home now?" she asked, hopeful.

"I need to talk to the doctor. I'll be back."

She never came back.

Sonja and Mitch didn't talk as they waited. He silently prayed that the doctors would see how badly Sonja needed this hospitalization, and he knew she was silently praying they wouldn't. *This needs to work*, Mitch thought.

The door opened. A man and two security guards entered the room. Sonja immediately stood up.

"We have a physician's evaluation certificate with your name on it, Mrs. Wasden. We are admitting you to the psychiatric hospital," the man stated calmly but firmly.

Mitch let out a breath he hadn't realized he was holding. Her dad was right; the plan worked. And God was sending more help, help that he, his wife, and his children needed. He felt like a ton of bricks had been lifted from his shoulders, and it felt good. It felt like relief.

"I refuse to go," Sonja fervently declared. And just like that, the ton of bricks came crashing back down on him. "Let's go home." She grabbed Mitch's arm. He looked at her and said nothing. He was done fighting. "Mitch, take me home," she pleaded. He could feel her panic and vulnerability.

"Mrs. Wasden, we're going to help you get well," the man insisted.

"But I'm not sick. I'm stressed! Why won't anyone believe me?" She was becoming hysterical. Mitch knew that Sonja couldn't see through the pain, and even though everyone around her could, she wouldn't let them lead her out of it.

"There is a van outside waiting to take you," the man stated. The two security guards were intently staring at Sonja. She turned to the man.

"You can't force me. I won't go!" she shouted at him.

"You're under the care of a physician, and he makes all the decisions for you. So, yes, we can force you. And we will." He held the door open for her.

The doctors were admitting Sonja no matter what, and in doing so Mitch felt his prayers had *finally* been answered.

"You're making a big mistake. I'm not sick!" She fought back.

"Mrs. Wasden, you're actually very sick," the man responded.

"I am not crazy!" she screamed.

He stood right in front of her and folded his arms. "No one is saying you're crazy, Mrs. Wasden."

This word, *crazy*, held so much power, and Mitch felt the urge to scream, "We are *all crazy!*" He certainly had felt many times like he was barely hanging on to his own sanity.

"Yet you're forcing me into the psych ward." Sonja reached out and grabbed Mitch's arm again and started shaking him.

Sonja, the Sonja he had fallen in love with, was waging a war inside herself, one that he had fought right along with her. They were battle worn, scarred, and bruised—but this was a battle they were obviously losing. He was desperate to save her.

He wrapped his arms around her. "You can do this. Things will be better, I promise. The sooner you go, the sooner you'll get to come home to the kids and me," he whispered in her ear.

"Please don't make me do this. I can get better without going to the hospital; I promise. I'll do yoga or deep breathing. Please!" she shamelessly begged.

"Look at me, Sonja," he softly asked. She slowly looked up into his eyes. He needed her to see the reasoning behind all this. "Please go. This could *save us*."

He watched her eyes change from desperation to strength. As he held her in his arms, he felt the very power she was gathering within her very being as all her trembling ceased. She gently put her hand on his face and placed a kiss on his cheek.

"For you, Mitch, and only you," she quietly said, then calmly walked out the door.

At the end of it all, Mitch knew Sonja, and Sonja would always choose them, her family, her tribe.

Mitch stood in the doorway, unable to take his eyes off his beautiful Sonja, walking full of fortitude down that long hospital hallway with one guard on each side of her and the man leading the way. Nurses and patients hovered around the scene and pretended not to stare, but they did. She didn't look back, not once. She kept walking that hospital hallway and out the doors with valor.

He looked down at his hands and realized he was holding papers he had no memory of getting. He saw they were instructions on having a loved one in the psychiatric hospital. Mitch knew he had won this battle, but the war was far from over. Would Sonja get a diagnosis? And most importantly, would she accept getting one?

CHAPTER 23

Drugged

Mitch nervously stood at the entrance doors to the psych ward along with other people waiting for the guards to buzz them in for visiting hours. He wasn't sure what Sonja would say to him. It wasn't clear if she believed this was the answer to getting her well or if she saw it as a box she needed to check before coming home.

The doors opened, and people headed to the common area, where patients were waiting for their visitors. Mitch searched for Sonja, but she was nowhere to be seen. He looked around the room, wondering if she had decided not to come. Had she decided to divorce him for forcing her into the psych ward?

Mitch wandered the halls until he saw Sonja's name written on a closed door. He carefully opened the door and saw Sonja sound asleep in her bed. He quietly walked in and sat in a chair by her bed.

"Sonja?" he gently said, trying to wake her up. Her eyes slowly opened but then fell immediately shut.

"Sonja?" he said again as he lightly shook her shoulder.

She tried to reach for him, but her arms fell back onto the mattress. He saw her lips moving, but no words came out.

"Are you okay?" he asked, realizing she wasn't asleep, she was drugged.

A nurse came in. "No one's allowed in patient rooms except doctors. You need to leave," she said impatiently.

"She's completely drugged." Mitch waved a hand over Sonja's body.

"The doctor put her on an antipsychotic that makes her sleepy. She'll be fine, but you need to leave this room," she said with authority as she walked out.

Mitch placed a kiss on Sonja's hand and started to leave.

"W-a-i-t," Sonja muttered, but the word came out slowly. She tried grabbing onto his shirt and fumbled out of bed. Mitch helped her up. Sonja went in and out of consciousness as he held her. She kept slipping through his fingers, sliding like a rag doll to the floor until she lay completely asleep on the tile. Mitch bent down and pulled her up into his arms.

The nurse came back into the room again. "Put her down!" she snapped. Two other nurses quickly came and took Sonja from Mitch's arms.

"Are you sure you're not overmedicating her?" Mitch felt a wave of panic.

"Her dose is determined by the doctor." The nurse brushed him off.

"But she can't even open her eyes," he said, frustrated.

"You need to leave, sir." She shooed Mitch out of the room and closed the door behind them.

Mitch headed straight for the front desk. "What medicine are you giving my wife? I'm concerned about the side effects. She can barely open her eyes," Mitch asked a man busily filling out a patient's chart.

"No need for concern. I can assure you it's a safe drug." The man closed the chart.

"I'm on list of people who can have access to Sonja's medical records. Can you tell me the *name* of each drug you're giving her?"

"Lamictal and Geodon. Geodon's what's making her sleepy."

"Does this mean she has a diagnosis?" Mitch asked eagerly.

The man behind the desk looked up at Mitch. "You need to trust the doctors. Allow them to do their job."

"Okay. But don't give her Geodon until after visiting hours so I am able to talk with her."

"I'll check with the doctors to see if we can get approval."

"Why is that not your procedure already? What's the point of visiting hours if the patient can't be visited?"

"I told you I would submit your request," he said, irritated.

At the hospital Mitch ran, he had often made visits to patients. The difference in how patients with physical illnesses were treated compared to the psych patients was astronomical. As Mitch walked to his car, he wished his hospital had a psych ward he could have put Sonja in. The fact that this unit was well staffed and that she would be safe gave him some reassurance, but he began to worry that being in the psych hospital may carry its own kind of collateral trauma that could be hard to get over.

CHAPTER 24

Visiting Hours

Sonja's dad flew back to Utah for work, but her mom stayed. Sonja's sister Allyson flew in to help with the kids while Mitch was at work. Mitch felt immense gratitude for the support they offered so freely and without judgment. They were able to keep the kids' schedule of tennis, schoolwork, tutors, and art lessons on track, to give the kids a sense of normalcy. Allyson made dinner every night, and the kids were in awe of the meals she made.

"Did you know Aunt Allyson can make bread without a recipe?" Rachael told Mitch as he was tucking her and the boys into bed.

"Chocolate-chip cookies too," Alex chimed in.

"She's definitely talented." Mitch grinned.

"I like Mom's cooking better," Lincoln huffed.

"Um, Mom doesn't cook," Alex contradicted.

"And that's just fine. Everyone has different talents." Mitch sat on the end of the bed. "What's important is that we all develop our individual interests. And you know what makes life even better?" he asked. They looked at him attentively.

"Enjoying other people's gifts. When I hear Mozart's Serenade No. 10 for Winds, it moves my soul every time. It makes me appreciate musicians even though I'm not one."

"I want to hear it," Rachael said.

"Yeah, play it for us." Alex sat up.

Mitch got his iPod out and attached it to Rachael's speaker.

Within seconds, the large bedroom was filled with oboes, clarinets, and bassoons. The kids stayed silent as the melody rolled through the space, and Mitch could feel the music pull his emotions out of his chest until they too were under Mozart's control. Rising and falling with every flick of his conductor's wand until they were completely silenced.

"That's my favorite song too," Alex said at the end.

"Of course it is." Rachael smirked. "If it's Dad's favorite, then it'll be yours too."

"I still like Mom's cooking better," Lincoln said.

"That's because she buys Taco Bell, and we all know you love their burritos," Alex said.

"When's Mom coming home from the hospital?" Lincoln asked Mitch.

"Soon," Mitch answered.

"Is she very sick?" Lincoln asked, worried.

Alex instantly pulled out a book and pretended to read for the rest of the conversation.

"She'll be back so quick, you'll forget she was ever gone." Mitch smiled.

"I miss her." Lincoln teared up.

"We all miss her," Mitch said as he kissed each one of their foreheads. Even though they all had their own bedrooms, they slept in the same king-size bed every night—Lincoln on the left side, Alex on the right, and Rachael at the foot of the bed. He stood at the door and looked over his little tribe before turning off the lights.

Mitch excelled at compartmentalizing his life. He succeeded as a hospital CEO and was known for his calm demeanor. As a father, he spent all his free time nurturing his children. His sick wife not only had his heart but his full attention. Mitch exhibited unflinching faith in his beliefs. He had read his scriptures and prayed every night since he was fourteen years old and hadn't missed a night since. Not one of these areas was allowed to bleed into any other. He was under the illusion that he could keep them from touching each other. He did not develop the skill of compartmentalizing consciously, but rather as a defense mechanism. Suppressing his thoughts and emotions was as automatic as breathing.

Mitch was going to be late.

"Nancy, I'll have to reschedule this meeting." Mitch rushed past his personal assistant.

"Oh, what day should I try and move it to?" She leaned over her desk as he ran out of the office.

"Just, any day," he hurriedly called back to her. He rushed to his car and sped to the psychiatric hospital. Visiting hours had already started. "Crap. She's gonna be pissed." He said the words out loud as he yanked his tie off.

Once in the parking lot, he parked the car and quickly took his suit coat off and threw it on the passenger seat. Would she even remember he had visited her the other night when she was drugged? He jogged to the front doors and waited for a guard to buzz him in.

The massive doors opened, and there was Sonja. Her eyes locked on him before she started running toward him with a smile so bright, it caused Mitch to abruptly stop walking. *Was she smiling?* He tried to do a double take as Sonja barreled right into him. He tried to pull her away to get another look at her face. He wanted to make sure his mind wasn't tricking him, but she wouldn't let go. She snuggled closer into his neck, and he held her as carefully as someone holding a priceless piece of porcelain.

Even though Mitch hoped the hospital would help her go back to the way she was when they were first married, it had been so long since he interacted with that girl, he wasn't sure how.

"Sonja, let's sit down. How are you feeling?"

"Take me home with you." She hugged him tighter.

"You'll be home soon," he said, walking them to the nearest couch. As they sat, she rested her head on his shoulder, and he stacked his head on top of hers. In silence, they stayed glued in that position, enjoying not being separated. With Sonja snuggled into him, she acted like this was their normal, like they had openly loved each other this whole time and today was no different. He felt a small bubble of hope push inside his chest. The constant tension and exhaustion that radiated from her had disappeared. Was it the medicine? Or was it all the extra sleep? Is this how she would behave from now on? This hospitalization held all of Mitch's hopes, yet he knew there was no guarantees.

After a while, Sonja looked up at him. "What's going to happen to us?"

"I don't know." He combed his fingers through her hair. "But we'll be okay." He rested his head back on hers, relishing the moment. It had been so long since he could sit with Sonja in loving silence that he wasn't ready to give it up just yet.

"Visiting hours are over," a nurse came from the front desk to inform them. Mitch saw a flash of concern on Sonja's face, like she was worried he might not come back.

"I want to go home with you." She panicked.

"You'll be home soon." He kissed her softly.

She waited by the doors as he walked himself out. Feeling her gaze on his back, Mitch stopped and turned around. They stood facing each other as the massive doors slowly began to shut between them. Mitch waved to her one last time, right as the large metal doors closed and locked. He stood in front of those closed doors, in his dark navy suit pants, crisp white shirt, and leather oxfords, staring at his leather watch but not really seeing the time. An overwhelming feeling of hope swelled inside him as his thoughts swirled in a million different places. The hospital was actually helping her.

CHAPTER 25

The Diagnosis

Mitch sat in the psych ward's family meeting room along with Sonja's mom and the counselor, Jane. It was time to share the doctor's diagnosis of Sonja. It had been a long six days for everyone—Sonja, the doctors, Mitch, the kids, Sonja's mom, and Allyson. As soon as Sonja was escorted into the room and sat down next to Mitch, the counselor got right to it.

"Sonja is mentally ill; she's bipolar." Jane pursed her lips.

Finally, a clear diagnosis! He had been trying to get a clear diagnosis from a professional for over a decade, and the day had finally come. Mitch would later find out his situation wasn't all that uncommon. A survey by the National Depressive and Manic-Depressive Association reported almost 70 percent of people with bipolar disorder are initially misdiagnosed, and more than one-third remain misdiagnosed for ten years or longer.[2]

Sonja's mental illness didn't show up one day and display all the symptoms at once for family members or doctors to evaluate. They appeared in fragmented pieces that built so gradually that over time Mitch got used to his new normal, not entirely grasping the stark difference from where he began to now. For years, he wondered what had tugged them off course, but now, he and

---

2 Singh T. Singh & Rajput, M. (2006). Misdiagnosis of Bipolar Disorder. *Psychiatry* (Edgmont), 3(10), 57–63.

Sonja both knew. Bipolar disorder. Mitch sat stunned as elation swept over him. Then Sonja's booming voice rang in his ears.

"What the hell do you mean I'm bipolar?"

With those words he felt Sonja was burning their own personal victory flag, after all this work, he feared they might be back at square one. Mitch snapped out of his elation and felt a knot tightening in the pit of his stomach.

"You, Jane, have known me for six days. Have we even had a proper conversation, a real heart-to-heart?" Sonja paused as fury spread across her face. "No, we haven't," she said, answering for Jane.

Mitch knew in that moment that he couldn't go home with the person sitting next to him. If Sonja didn't accept that she was bipolar, the diagnosis meant nothing.

"Sonja!" her mom tried interrupting, but she couldn't be stopped.

"How irresponsible of you, labeling me mentally ill. Are you even a doctor? Are you qualified to make that diagnosis?" She suddenly turned to Mitch. "You don't think I'm mentally ill, do you?"

He knew that was a loaded question. Sonja reminded him of a spooked horse, and as much as he wanted to stand up and yell, "Yes, yes, I do!" Instead he said, "I don't know," trying to strike a diplomatic tone.

"Your doctor diagnosed you as bipolar, Sonja. You *are* mentally ill," Jane said for clarification.

"Where's my doctor? Why is he not telling me my diagnosis? A real classy place you've got here. Real professional, Jane," Sonja fought back.

Mitch did wonder why they wouldn't go get one of her doctors. But he knew he had to trust the professionals, since this was the first step to getting a person as reluctant as Sonja to begin processing the news.

"It's a lifelong illness; you have to accept it." Jane got firm.

"What if I don't? You think you're going to hand me a life sentence without a peep from me? Not a chance in hell!" she stood up and screamed.

The stigma around being mentally ill was so bad that Sonja was willing to reject the diagnosis instead of walking the path that would get her well.

"This family meeting is over!" Jane yelled, completely fed up. "You're not leaving here until you accept it. Do you hear me? You're not leaving this hospital until you admit you're bipolar!" She opened the door. "Nurses, come get Sonja."

It was devastating, watching Sonja thrashing around in attempts to resist the nurses trying to escort her out of the room. When Sonja grabbed onto Mitch's arm, it took all of his power to stand there motionless as the nurses were forcefully pulling her off him. She kicked and screamed, and Mitch stood there watching. He learned that doing absolutely nothing in that moment was one of the greatest tests of pure grit he had ever faced.

"Mitch, you've got to help me! Don't let them get away with this!" Sonja screamed.

He desperately wanted to grab Sonja, wrap her in his arms, and take her home. She had been through enough, and calling it a day felt right. But all these instincts and urges had to be clamped down. He stood as still as possible, his jaw clenched. He knew if he truly wanted to help his wife, he needed to let this play out.

"Mitch, this place is terrible! Stop them!" she cried out.

He choked back tears as two nurses grabbed her wrists and forced her through the door.

One of Sonja's greatest battles was being fought inside of her, and for the first time in their marriage, he sent her out there to fight it alone. As much as he wished this would just all go away, he knew he wouldn't sign any of Sonja's release papers until she accepted she was bipolar.

That night, Mitch sat on the couch in the psych ward, waiting for Sonja, rubbing his sweaty hands together. They informed him that after the disastrous family meeting Sonja had been taken to a de-escalation room, a padded cell. She stayed locked up for hours because she wouldn't stop pounding on the door and screaming. Eventually they let her out because her doctor said that was enough and he would handle the situation. Mitch knew that Sonja craved freedom, and not only did she need to radically accept she had the bipolar disorder, she also needed to find some type of freedom within it.

Mitch waited while Sonja was discussing her diagnosis with her doctor. He paced the waiting room, playing out how the conversation might be going between them. After blurry, panic-filled minutes passed by Mitch looked up and saw Sonja slowly walking toward him. She stopped once she stood toe to toe with him, yet she didn't touch him. Despite her chin being high in the air her eyes showed fear.

"Fine. I'll accept I'm bipolar," she declared as her voice shook.

"Really?" Mitch looked at her.

She sat down elegantly at the edge of a bench and turned to him, eyes blazing. Her eyes were the most fascinating part of Sonja. They were like the weather, constantly changing.

"My question is, are you willing to fight this illness with me?" she asked.

He took her hands. "When have I not fought your battles with you?"

"Yesterday," she replied with her back stiff, not touching the wall.

"And before yesterday?"

"Never."

"Then you should know you don't need to ask. I'll stand by your side." He kissed her fingers, which were ice cold.

"I know if I want to keep my family, I have to acknowledge that I have a mental illness," she admitted.

"That's definitely a step in the right direction."

"My twenty-year-old self is grieving the life I thought I'd have. I have spent so much energy dreaming and planning my future; I was so excited for it. I never thought this would be where I ended up. My dreams have all gone up in smoke."

"Letting things burn isn't always destructive. Sometimes letting something go up in flames is cleansing. Gives you a fresh start," he said trying to reframe their situation.

"I just need time."

CHAPTER 26

Coming Home

The next morning, Mitch stood once again in front of the psych ward doors, waiting for them to open. He held a bouquet of cream-colored roses, Sonja's favorite. She was coming home, and Mitch felt slightly nervous about bringing her back. Even though he had spent hours researching bipolar disorder, he didn't feel any more prepared to take on an illness with such magnitude. While doctors had brought them this far, his confidence in the mental health field had still been greatly shaken.

While reading about bipolar, the words "avoid antidepressants" came up several times. The very antidepressants the doctors had been giving Sonja for years actually made her bipolar worse. Many antidepressants trigger manic episodes. At the time, Mitch thought her sudden mood switches were a positive sign, when in reality it was bringing out a different side to the illness. Now Mitch could clearly see that a lot of Sonja's behaviors, like playing the stock market or her never-ending ideas, were manic.

Thoughts about the past, the present, and the future were all getting tangled together like a big messy ball of yarn. All he knew for certain was Sonja, her bipolar disorder, their marriage, and their kids all had to figure out a way to live together.

The doors buzzed open, and Sonja excitedly rushed to Mitch.

"Ready to go home?" He hugged her.

"Yes, please!" She gripped him tightly. He leaned back and handed her the roses.

"Thank you, Mitch." She smiled as she breathed in the bouquet.

"I've missed you." He tenderly kissed her. Sonja pulled away just a few inches, and their eyes met as Sonja touched her forehead to his. Mitch could get lost in Sonja's eyes, which held so much emotion. Moments like these were sacred to him. This powerful bond to Sonja was inexplicable.

"Let's go." He took her hand. As they walked toward their car, he grabbed a loop on her jeans and held on to it.

Sonja's mom, her sister Allyson, and all three of their kids were waiting for Sonja when she walked into the house. Sonja instantly dropped her bag and opened her arms wide. The kids rushed into them. They were not allowed to visit Sonja in the psych ward and had greatly missed her. No matter how dysfunctional things had gotten, the kids desperately wanted their mother's love back in their lives.

Mitch put his arms around his family. "It's good to have you back," he said.

"You don't look tired anymore," Lincoln said, looking up at Sonja's eyes.

"I finally got to sleep." She smiled authentically—a smile the kids hadn't seen in a long time.

"Look what I drew while you were gone." Rachael flopped open her messy sketchbook to a drawing of a black bear catching a salmon.

Sonja tapped her finger on the bear. "We will have to get a frame for that one. It's good, like really good."

Alex cautiously took Sonja's hand. "Come look at the fort Dad and us made in the playroom," he said.

"Okay!" Sonja laughed as she followed the kids upstairs to their secret fort. She sat inside the fort with them and listened to their ideas, dreams, and friend problems as seriously as any adult's. She was not just a mom to them but their confidante. Having their grandma and aunt visit and take care of them was nice, but no one could replace their mom.

CHAPTER 27

Doctoral Program

While you are caring for someone with an illness, it often feels selfish to talk about your own needs and pain when the other person's needs and pain are so much greater than your own. Because Mitch was viewed by Sonja as the "healthy" one in their marriage, she relied on him to do more and be physically present if he wasn't at work. As a result, he had little time for hobbies and friends. When people at work discussed their weekend of playing golf, cycling, or training for half-marathons, he couldn't fathom how people fit those things into their lives.

He was grateful for one routine that got the family out of the house each Saturday. He and Sonja would take the kids to the AMC theater to see a movie. At the end of each movie, Mitch would analyze the movie's plot points with the kids. They would discuss character development and what could have made the film better. The analytical discussion was as much fun as the movie. Mitch enjoyed training his junior movie critics and storyline experts.

In the monthly hospital newsletter, Mitch would write movie reviews of all the films he had seen. It provided him a way to relate with people and have discussions about some of his interests.

Those Saturdays were the only socializing he ever did. He wanted more. He *needed* more. He felt the effects of emotional burnout and realized it was vital he refueled emotionally, or he wouldn't have anything to give Sonja or his family.

Mitch had a love of learning and read books on business leadership and neuroscience. For him, learning was something he could do when Sonja couldn't leave the house. It was his escape, a kind of life of the mind. Learning provided him a type of relief. So when Mitch's older brother Chris approached him about a doctoral program he was applying to and asked Mitch if he'd be interested in applying as well, he felt a flash of excitement.

Mitch was accepted and began the executive doctoral program at George Washington University, studying human and organizational learning. For four years, his schedule was tight, and every minute mattered. He stopped watching TV before bed and carried articles with him to read whenever he had a few spare minutes. Though stressful, the program opened his eyes to a community of scholars and conversations he hadn't known existed. Mitch learned about complexity/chaos theory, neuroscience, leadership, and learning theory. Most importantly, during the program Mitch discovered mindfulness while doing research for a paper. Mindfulness became the lens he would see his life through, and it saved him.

In his studies, he knew that mindfulness was often used by those with mental health challenges, and he tried many times unsuccessfully to talk to Sonja about it. Each of the books or CDs he offered her went unread and unlistened to.

One class period, Dr. Clyde Croswell, a professor who specialized in mindfulness, announced he'd be taking a group of students and one guest per person to Chile to study mindfulness and leadership.

As Mitch got into bed that night after his long flight home from Washington, DC, he gathered Sonja in his arms. "My doctoral program is going to Chile to study mindfulness, and we each get to bring a guest." Mitch wanted to share mindfulness with Sonja and wondered if this trip could be the key to get her to understand it.

"Are you inviting me on a trip to Chile?" She got excited.

"Yes."

"How romantic!" she teased.

"Will you go?"

"Of course!" She snuggled in closer.

The retreat began in the small village of Cuncumen, Chile, a mountain town of fifty residents. In the morning, they did yoga and meditated. In the afternoon, academics taught their group about mindfulness. During the trip, they traveled to Santiago to hear other lectures.

"What's next?" Sonja asked enthusiastically as they walked off their bus in Santiago.

"Another meditation session." Mitch led her to the meditation room, where everyone formed a circle as a mindfulness instructor led the group.

"Close your eyes and think of a flower," the instructor calmly said.

Mitch closed his eyes and exhaled through his nose, and the faintest image of a lilac began to take shape in his mind. He focused on the abstract flower and observed his feelings as they flowed through him. Fear. Anxiety. Peace. Frustration. Tranquility. Although it was a contradictory mix of emotions, through mindfulness, no matter what was going on around him, he could dissociate from those feelings. He didn't have to be his thoughts and experiences; he was enough just *being*. Mindfulness and meditation brought a peace to his life that gave him strength he had never had before. Mindfulness was a practice he could do and find inner peace, no matter what was going on in his external world.

"What color and shape is your flower?" their instructor asked.

Mitch's mind refocused on the petals of his lilac, and they filled with color.

"Now breathe in," the instructor continued.

Mitch inhaled deeply, feeling the oxygen bring life into his body, and the stem and leaves took form.

"And out." The instructor finished the cycle. "Now open your eyes."

Everyone opened their eyes.

"Let's explore how we visualize language differently." The instructor continued, "I may say *flower*, and to me, that may mean *red rose*, but to you, it might mean *white daisy*. Language creates mental maps. Let us see what flower everyone's map brought them."

The instructor began going around the room, having everyone share what type of flower they had visualized. Mitch turned around smiling when it was time for Sonja to share.

"Umm," she said looking perplexed at everyone in the room.

"Just clear your mind and close your eyes," the instructor said, trying to help Sonja see her flower.

Sonja quickly squeezed her eyes tight. "Ahh. Yes," she said as she slightly opened one eye, peering at the instructor, who was patiently waiting.

"That's it," the instructor encouraged.

"A rose. It's white." Sonja opened her eyes, grinning, thinking she had fooled everyone, which she probably had, but not Mitch.

"The point of this guided meditation is that we each create our own realities in our mind, even when we hear the same word. Always question the reality your mind creates. Is that reality useful? Is there a different story you could tell yourself that is equally true and more helpful to you?" The instructor smiled. "And most importantly, realize that you are not your thoughts."

It was hard for Mitch to not notice Sonja was unable to access the lessons being taught, despite her enthusiasm and efforts. He wondered if it was because her mind and emotions were constantly moving at such rapid speeds that it simply wasn't possible for her to meditate. Mitch had wanted mindfulness to save Sonja, the way it had saved him.

"I think we're done for the day," Mitch said to Sonja, taking her by the arm as they walked toward the evening sunset. It felt so easy to be with her in that moment. She had an arm wrapped around Mitch's waist.

Sonja seemed happier than he'd seen her in a long time. She was taking antipsychotics that definitely stabilized her moods, but not without a cost. The side effects, dizziness, drowsiness (sometimes to the point where Sonja was unable to stay awake), generalized weakness, headaches, and a feeling of restlessness to the point where, at times, she couldn't sit still, were now a part of Sonja's daily life. She would often pace for hours, and because she wanted to be a part of the kids' and Mitch's fun, the hallway by the playroom was her favorite one to pace. Mitch admired her commitment to taking her medicine and coping with the many side effects.

Sonja was also doing individual therapy along with being a part of a daily outpatient program where they held classes for patients to learn how to cope with stressors and manage their mental health. For now, Mitch was satisfied and had to believe that things would continue to get better.

CHAPTER 28

The Job Search

2010

A set of paradoxical needs existed in Mitch. One was a need to create stability for Sonja, and the other was an unquenchable passion for growth. Unfortunately, the two rarely coexisted well. After Mitch had been working for four years in Baton Rouge, a recruiter called him about a new job opportunity in Lubbock, Texas, and after discussing it with Sonja, he turned in his résumé to the recruiter.

Mitch's search process for a new job could easily take four to eight months, with three to four interviews. It was not uncommon for a recruiter to begin with one hundred–plus applicants, then narrow the field to a slate of ten to twelve candidates to share with their client. That slate would be reduced to four to five candidates to be invited for interviews, until the final candidate was selected.

The process always began with excitement, but as the uncertainty of the search processes unfolded, it left Sonja completely unhinged. It often seemed that they were doomed to keep repeating the same cycle.

"Stop talking!" Sonja screamed from the couch.

Mitch sat in the kitchen, and the clinking of his spoon in a cereal bowl chimed behind her sobs.

"You can take your next wife on all your career journeys. I did most of it; the end part will be easy. Like my sister Allyson says, it is so predictable with my illness; it gets like this every time you job search! I *just* need stability!"

"Sonja, then let's drop out of the search," he calmly stated.

"No. We are not doing that! Just stop talking, Mitch!" Her face went red, and they sat in silence while she caught her breath. "You do not understand." She desperately looked at him.

"Sonja, I understand you feel overwhelmed, but you can't say you feel miserable being in a search and then refuse to get out of it," Mitch said.

"Oh my gosh! Please stop!" She jerked her head back toward the kitchen. "There is only one way out of this. I should just end my life. I sit here and think, 'Why did I keep fighting this illness for so long?' I mean, really, for what? To suffer more later? I can't do a normal life; I can't even have you in a job search without getting suicidal." She sobbed.

"Sonja, you're more important to me than a job search. I'm withdrawing from the search." Mitch had decided.

"No! You're not hearing me! Our choices are killing me!" She got quiet and wiped her tears before looking back at him. "It's the moving, the instability of our life that has just been *sucking* it out of me. And I take ownership of those decisions. Do you?" She blew her nose with a wet tissue.

Mitch carefully chose his next words. "Sonja, what's hard is that in the many times we've moved, you've said you've prayed about it and felt like we should be moving, but then in moments like this, you say every move has been a mistake. I can't have you agree we should move and then have you say it's all a mistake, because I can't undo that decision."

"Ugh, see." She dropped her hand on her lap. "You bring God into it. See!" She pointed at him. "You always bring God into it!"

"Sonja, you've told me you have felt we should move many times." Mitch sighed.

"No! Just *stop*!" she yelled. "I refuse to believe God wanted this for me, because that makes me think he must want me dead!" She let out a big breath. "It was all a mistake, Mitchell."

"Ugh. Would you just *stop*!" he yelled in frustration. "We come back to this over and over again, but you never—"

"Oh, we're 'back to this'? Hello? You think I don't know that! You don't think I feel it coursing through my body every time we end up here again? Oh no, I'm just completely clueless. Just *stop*! Stop talking. Just keep living your life. I don't care what you tell your next wife about me. Tell her I was vicious. Tell her I was a nightmare. But I am a hundred percent clear on what is taking my life—your career!" She started pacing back and forth.

He tried being softer. "You are a very strong person, Sonja, and I'm sorry our life choices have been so hard on you."

"You can say whatever you want, but I don't think people are stupid. At my funeral, everyone will know what took me down. It's not like it will take a genius."

"Sweetheart," he said more gently. She ignored him. "Sonja, I can pull out of the job search. Our family is more important." Mitch gathered her in his arms.

"No! I want you to stay in it. We're already this close, and you might get it!" she pleaded with him.

"Sonja, I think I should pull out; this is making you sick again," he said, worried.

"If you pull out, I swear I will divorce you. I will always *wonder* if we would have been the ones chosen to get the job."

"Sonja, maybe it's okay to wonder," he said.

"It will torture me!"

"It already is!" he said, exasperated.

"We need to see this through! Don't pull out! I will never forgive you!" She squeezed two wads of tissue in each hand.

"Things will be okay. Let's just have faith that if we do our best, the right thing will happen." He tried reassuring her. "What's for you won't go past you."

Would he give up his career ambitions for Sonja's life? Of course. But he had no way of knowing what Sonja really wanted versus what her illness demanded. So, he decided to stay in the search.

At home, it never seemed to matter how hard he worked; things didn't seem to get much better. Mitch craved a sense of progress in his life, and work was the one place he achieved that. At work, he gained enormous satisfaction by working hard with a team and seeing results.

When Mitch arrived at Ochsner Medical Center in Baton Rouge, they were losing money and had the worst patient and employee satisfaction in the hospital system. During his time there, he focused relentlessly on improving the culture of the hospital, and after four years, the hospital was profitable and had the highest employee engagement and patient satisfaction in the hospital system. Their quality scores even tied for first with the flagship hospital. Mitch's career aspirations started out of money insecurity but had developed into something so much more. He had sacrificed so many things for Sonja, yet his career ambitions had not been one of them. And his career was the one thing that was his and his alone.

CHAPTER 29

Unexpected News

About four months later, Mitch sat at his office desk, processing the exciting news the recruiter had just shared with him when his phone rang. It was Sonja.

"I was just about to call you. I made it to the final two for the Lubbock, Texas, job!" he said, exhilarated.

"Mitch, you'll never believe it: a Realtor called me and said someone wants to buy our house—and we didn't even have it for sale!" Sonja's shocked voice rang through the phone.

Upon their arrival in Louisiana, Sonja had bought a fixer-upper with the hope of flipping it after renovations were completed. It had been on the market for three long years. The constant stress of being kicked out of the house at a moment's notice for a Realtor to show it to a buyer became wearing, which is why they took it off the market and decided to stay in it while they lived in Baton Rouge. To have a buyer now seemed surreal.

"Seriously?" Mitch said, taken aback.

"Mitch, this job in Lubbock is meant to be! God is paving the way for us," Sonja excitedly said.

"The recruiter said they want us to fly out for the on-site interview," Mitch informed Sonja.

"Mitch, I'm so ready for this!"

When they landed, Lubbock was as hot and humid as the Texas Sonja and Mitch had remembered. Mitch interviewed all day while a Realtor took Sonja to look at houses. By the end of the day, Mitch felt the interviews went extremely well but knew nothing was for sure until he had the offer. Sonja, on the other hand, felt they were official Texans again. A car dropped them off at the airport to fly home, and Mitch answered all of Sonja's burning questions about how the interviews went as they rolled their small suitcase through the airport.

"What did the recruiter say about how you did?"

"He told me to prepare for an offer, which would be amazing."

"The recruiter told you to prepare for an offer?" Sonja jumped in eagerness.

"You need to understand it's a recruiter's job to sell candidates the positions they are trying to fill," he cautiously said.

"I found the *perfect* house! It has all my colors, creams and whites, with dark wood. I can't wait to move in!"

"It's still fifty-fifty," he cautiously guided her enthusiasm back to reality.

"No, you're getting this job." She laughed. "Our house is selling; you just made it to the final two. It's obvious divine intervention has taken place." She let out an excited sigh. "The buyers want us out of the house in three weeks. I found a cheap two-bedroom five-hundred-square-foot apartment for us to move into."

"I don't think that's smart." Mitch shook his head.

"Just think, if you do get the job, we don't want a house we have to sell."

"We could just rent a house," he suggested.

"No, no, no." She got firm. "You're getting the job, and we'll be moving soon. This apartment makes more sense."

"We can't fit all our stuff in that tiny of an apartment, Sonja." Mitch found her logic a bit humorous.

"Then we'll get a storage unit." She shot her eyes at him.

Mitch's reluctance about putting everything into storage and living in a five-hundred-square-foot apartment didn't slow Sonja down for one second. They put almost everything they owned into storage and moved into the two-bedroom apartment. Rachael and Lincoln slept in bunk beds, and Alex slept on a couch. Even though they could afford to rent a house or a bigger apartment, Sonja wanted to save money. Mitch could never figure out how Sonja calculated money in her head. They would eat at a nice restaurant, and she would order the most expensive thing on the menu but refuse to order a drink because it was too expensive.

His family camped out in the small apartment, waiting to hear when they'd be moving to Lubbock, and several weeks later, Mitch came home with news.

"The recruiter called." He sat down with a heavy heart. "I didn't get the job," he said, not knowing what reaction he would get from Sonja.

She stared at him, dumbfounded. "God must hate us," Sonja sharply whispered as devastation spread across her face.

"No, Sonja. The other candidate is God's child too. The job was meant for him and his family." Mitch took her trembling hands in his.

Sonja pushed his hands away.

Mitch knew this disappointment was going to further deepen Sonja's faith crisis. Her God questions were often targeted at Mitch, but he felt like an inadequate spokesman for God. His answers were no wiser or more profound than what he had learned as a child in Sunday school. God loves us. We are his children. God's ways are not always our ways. But none of those answers brought Sonja comfort. That idea that God's will might include seemingly intolerable emotional pain was unfathomable to her, and because this pain was brought on by Mitch not getting the job, he felt like he had let her down.

Most mental illnesses are not cured but managed, and Mitch and Sonja had not acquired the skill set to manage a disappointment this large. Unbeknownst to them, a tragic life event was coming that would start an uncontrollable forest fire.

CHAPTER 30

The Phone Call

February 8, 2011

Mitch sat with the kids at the dinner table in their tiny apartment. He was staring at a warmed-up Stouffer's lasagna in the claustrophobic kitchen when his phone rang.

"Hey, Heidi."

"Mitch, I need to talk to Sonja; it's urgent. Opa killed himself." He went silent, and in a state of complete shock, automatically handed Sonja the phone. "It's your sister," he whispered. The kids took bites of their lasagna, unaware of the tragic news being shared on the other end.

Sonja collapsed on the floor and let out a terrifying scream. The kids jumped and looked at Mitch. He picked the phone up off the ground.

"Heidi, we'll call you later." He hung up.

"No, no, no, no!" Sonja screamed.

"What's wrong?" Rachael asked, frightened.

"He shot himself!" Sonja cried.

"Who?" Alex asked.

"Opa! Opa shot himself," Sonja shouted. She curled up in a tight ball on the floor and frantically began rocking back and forth, howling in pain.

The kids went silent, and Mitch worried what insecurities this would put into their minds. Sonja was very open about her suicidal thoughts, and his concern was the kids would worry she would die next. He gathered his kids in his arms, not knowing what to say. How does a person talk about suicide? How would he navigate giving David the respect, compassion, and love he deserved without driving deeper into Sonja that suicide was an acceptable option? His heart and mind couldn't begin to comprehend how to discuss it, so he said nothing, giving the moment the silence it needed. In his heart, he had to believe Sonja would never die by suicide.

They all attended David's funeral later that week. Mitch watched Sonja walk to the podium in the packed church as she spoke of the great love she had for her father. In the middle of her own emotional fire, she found the grit to compose herself for this tribute to her father. Mitch was once again reminded of her strength and felt proud to be her husband.

He held Sonja's hand as everyone gathered around David's casket at the gravesite. He was haunted by what this could do to her. Her father was her safe place; a person she could call when she was in her darkest moments, someone who could make her feel loved. Sonja leaned heavily on her dad, and now he was gone. Mitch had relied on David as a partner in treating Sonja's illness, and now that support was gone.

As the months went by, Sonja cried incessantly, rarely talked, and refused to leave her bed. She took her medications, continued to see her psychiatrist and therapist, which allowed her to keep her nose only slightly above the waterline. At times like this, when Sonja was struggling, Mitch tried to be the buffer, the one who made the kids believe everything was normal.

"Sonja, come on, let's get you cleaned up and go to a movie," he said.

"I'm not going." She laid her cheek on a tear-stained pillow.

An Impossible Wife

"Sonja, it's becoming unhealthy for the kids to see all this. Please, just come." He sighed.

"Go without me." She tugged a blanket over her shoulders. "Go be happy without me!"

He stood by the bed, not touching her. "Something has to change," he said to the floor.

"What do you mean?" she asked, lifting her face up to see him.

"We've got to get out of this two-bedroom apartment and move on. We just lost your dad; we can't lose you too." He exhaled. The oppressive living situation they were in scared him. "The kids and I can't keep living this way." He turned and walked out. Mitch took the kids to the theater.

The challenge with mental illness and marriage is that people wrongly assume the healthy person is always functioning at 100 percent and should be able to make up the emotional deficits of the mentally ill spouse. The truth is that the mental health of both become linked. When Sonja was depressed, it often made Mitch depressed. When she overspent, he dealt with the aftermath. They rode the same emotional roller coaster. The sick are frontline soldiers in a brutal and unforgiving war. The healthy are the medics and bodyguards, putting themselves in harm's way to protect and heal the injured. The worse Sonja got, the worse Mitch got, and this time he needed Sonja's help to put their lives back together.

When Mitch and the kids came home from the movies, the apartment had been cleaned and Sonja had showered, was in fresh clothes, and had homes for sale pulled up on her computer. Clearly a switch had flipped somewhere within her.

"I called a Realtor. He's taking me to see some houses tomorrow," Sonja said like a woman on a mission.

Within weeks, they had bought a townhouse, unpacked, and gotten the kids into a private school. Sonja started showering regularly on her own, kept the house clean, took care of the kids' every need with no emotional outbursts, and continued to take her meds and go to therapy. The change came so suddenly that it was almost eerie.

The strangest thing was that she never mentioned her dad, her illness, her pain—and did not appear to be someone who was grieving. When Mitch looked into her eyes, they were flat. She had shoved her grief and illness somewhere deep down, but he couldn't figure out where she had placed it. When he came home from work and asked her what she had done all day, she would often reply, "Stared at the wall." Like it was a regular activity. And although he enjoyed this break from being her constant emotional support, he couldn't help but wonder if her sudden ability to function would come to haunt him.

CHAPTER 31

Ebay

Columbia, Missouri
2012

A recruiter called about a chief operating officer job at the University of Missouri Health Care System, and Mitch decided to apply but didn't tell Sonja. It was another grueling period of interviews and waiting, but Mitch was selected for the job. When he told Sonja about the offer, she was excited to be moving to Missouri for a fresh start.

They bought a comfortable home, enrolled the boys in great public schools, and got Rachael settled into college for her freshman year at BYU Idaho. The boys made an army of friends, and their house was deemed the party house, where Sonja provided loads of pizza and sodas. Sonja continued in her state of high functionality and insisted that things were fine for several years. But Mitch kept getting that strange, uneasy feeling a person gets before a hurricane comes—the calm before the storm—and that storm dripped one small eBay package at a time.

Mitch checked the mail and saw a white box addressed to Sonja. Mitch brought it in and set a stack of bills and magazines on the counter.

"This came for you." He handed Sonja the box.

"Thanks." She grabbed it.

"What is it?" he asked, tossing junk mail in the trash.

"Oh, just a little something I got off eBay on a deal. It's nothing." She took the box into the bedroom.

eBay boxes started arriving daily, making them impossible to ignore. Every time Mitch asked Sonja about it, she brushed him off. When he came home to six packages stacked at their front door, he grabbed a knife and sliced through the taped edges. He pulled a narrow red jewelry box out of the foam peanuts. As he cracked open the box, a thick gold bracelet lay on a cushion with a folded piece of paper tucked inside the top of the box. He read the receipt's amount, $2,000. Mitch looked at the other five packages and his stomach dropped. He opened them one by one; each package contained a gold bracelet of similar or greater value. Alarmed he carried the gold bracelets into the bedroom and set them on the bed in front of Sonja.

"What's all this?"

She looked up from her computer and froze. "I'm taking it back; just stop." She tensed up.

"What about the other seven boxes from last week?" he asked.

"I can't have you get mad at me today! Seriously, Mitchell, do you want me to lose it? Just don't go there!" She put up a firm hand to him.

"I'm not getting mad; I'm asking what this is." He pointed to the gold bracelets.

"You know what—no. You are not going to send me spiraling like that. I don't have to tell you. I'm taking them all back, so don't worry about it." She looked back at her laptop stubbornly.

"You're returning *all* of it?" he asked for clarification.

"Yes!" she yelled, put out.

A week later, Sonja walked into the kitchen with gold bracelets lining her wrists.

"I thought you returned those." Mitch raised his voice in disbelief.

"I will!" she snapped. "Now, real quick, which is prettier?" She held her arms out to him.

"Seriously?" He shook his head, incredulous.

"This one is the prettiest, isn't it?" She pointed to a thin gold bangle engraved with scrolling vines and flowers.

"I'm not doing this." He walked out of the kitchen, and she followed him.

"I just need to know which one is the most unique, stunning."

"If you're returning them, why does it matter?" he shouted.

"I'm just looking!" she shouted back.

"You're still shopping, aren't you?" He glared at her.

"I'll return all of them," she said, full of conviction, but their credit card statements rolled in with numbers that suggested otherwise.

In one month, she had spent $35,000 on jewelry, and there was no indication of any of them being returned. He threw the credit card statements onto the dining room table and went to track down Sonja. She was washing dishes. Mitch took one of her wrists and tried unclasping the gold bracelets she was wearing.

"What are you doing?" Sonja batted away his hands.

"I'm returning all the bracelets. Where are the rest?"

"I returned them." She yanked her arms from him.

"You're lying." He picked up her purse and took her wallet out. He removed every single one of her credit cards and put them into his pocket. "This isn't over." He stormed out and headed into their bedroom.

Mitch began searching her drawers and under the bed, where he excavated several pieces of jewelry. In the bedroom closet, he cleared off every shelf letting stacks of clothes fall around him as he found several diamond bracelets tucked between sweaters. Gripping the jewelry, he stepped around the clothes and headed back into their bedroom, surveying the room. Mitch went to the bed and lifted up the mattress and found a pile of credit cards with their statements. He had a brief moment of déjà vu, thinking of years earlier, when she had lost their savings in the stock market. Mitch started glancing through the credit card statements and saw many had his name on them. He just stood there like a statue. He was sure he was going to vomit. Sonja walked in the bedroom, saw Mitch, and tried to quickly leave.

"Why is my name on these?" He held the credit card bills in front of her face. "I didn't open these!" he yelled.

"I know, Mitch," she said. Her eyes were looking anywhere but into his.

"Explain it *now*," he snapped.

"I opened them in your name," she said, trembling.

"Sonja, you're clearly in a manic episode!"

"I can't stop it," she cried out, tears starting to pour down her face. "Please, help me!" She crumpled to the floor.

"Help? Help how?" He threw up his arms in the air.

"I can't control it!" she said in desperation.

"Then return the bracelets and cancel the credit cards!" he yelled, exhausted.

"I've tried, and I can't! I returned a bracelet, and my OCD had to find another one just like it. I spent two days on the computer looking for an identical match. It's driving me crazy!" she screamed back.

"You've got to talk to your psychiatrist," Mitch said, panicked.

The illness seemed to always be in the driver's seat, Mitch never knowing what road it would drive them down next. The next morning, when he went to return the jewelry, all the bracelets had disappeared. He knew Sonja had taken them, and given her current lack of lucidity, Mitch knew he needed professional advice on how to handle the situation. The credit card companies didn't care what had caused the charges—charges were charges, and they would demand to be paid.

CHAPTER 32

Lock Me Up

Columbia, Missouri
Fall 2015

Mitch drove home from work, not knowing which Sonja he would be facing. Due to her manic spending episode, her psychiatrist had been trying different medicine combinations to try to stabilize her, and with every new medicine, he got a different version of his wife. Altering medication meant there were new side effects with each one.

When he arrived home, he found Sonja throwing up in the toilet.

"This new medicine is making me feel like I have the flu." She wiped her mouth. "How was today?" she asked apprehensively.

They had been living under the same roof, even sleeping in the same bed, but they might as well have been living in different countries with how little they communicated. The tension in their marriage increased with each credit card statement rolling in at dangerously high numbers. Mitch realized that paying off her credit cards was not a permanent fix.

"Sonja, I'm not going to pay off the credit cards," he stated matter-of-factly.

"Fine. Whatever," Sonja said flatly. "I have bigger problems to worry about." She walked back to the bed lethargically and climbed under the covers. "They keep trying different medicines on me, and I feel like a lab rat."

Mitch sat on his side of the bed and took his shoes off, finding it difficult to warm up to her and be empathetic to her plight. "Becoming manic isn't your fault, but lying and hiding things from me is something entirely different," he said, shaking his head. Mitch wanted to hold her feet to the fire, but she ignored what he was saying.

"I'm having myself admitted to the psych ward. You'll need to take me," she abruptly informed him.

"What?" He turned to her in disbelief.

"I can't stop. I feel like I am on a runaway train," she cried out, tears starting to drench her face.

Mitch drove Sonja to Saint Mary's Hospital in Jefferson City, which was an hour away. It was the only psych ward with an open bed. He had seen the ins and outs of the mental health field and now realized the system was severely broken. The patients' demand for services often overwhelmed health-care providers and hospitals. There was a shortage of psychiatrists and psychologists, meaning that if someone was in crisis now, it could take one to three months to get an appointment. Whereas if someone had a sore throat, they could see a doctor that same day. Subsequently, the ER was constantly filled with people desperately needing mental health care.

Often, the mentally ill and their loved ones feel helpless and hopeless. But Mitch knew he needed hope to get through this, so he hoped for the best and prepared himself for the worst. He took Sonja's name off the house, the cars, his bank account, all his credit cards, and anything that would provide her a way to access money. During the week that she was in the hospital, he bought a safe where he would lock all checks, credit cards, and his wallet. Mitch wondered if Sonja would get off that runaway train, and if she did, what stop they would end up at next.

CHAPTER 33

Therapy

Mitch waited for his therapist in the outdated office that tried so desperately to look homey, anxiously awaiting the advice he couldn't give himself. He glanced at the bookshelf and realized he had read many of the books on that shelf in an attempt to help Sonja and to understand his own internal struggles.

Sonja and his mental health struggles had caused him to be intrigued by the mental maps humans use to, in essence, create reality in the brain. He spent hours talking about these concepts with fellow doctoral students and professors. Mitch wondered how to apply these theories in the business world. His interests had gone beyond reading, and he and his brother Chris had coauthored two books on the neuroscience of organizational culture and innovation. Both books received endorsements from Fortune 500 CEOs and thought leaders, but in light of his current situation, none of his knowledge seemed to matter.

"How are things going?" His therapist walked in smiling.

"They've been better," he said wearily. "Sonja went on a manic spending spree and is in the psych ward."

The therapist motioned for him to continue.

"She took credit cards out in my name without me knowing and racked up thousands of dollars of charges. One card alone has $20,000 on it."

The therapist let out a low whistle. "Wow." He continued to

scribble down notes. Mitch often thought about the stacks and stacks of files therapists and doctors had on his family that all seemed for naught.

"She also wrote down my credit card numbers when I was in the shower. The bills just keep rolling in." He sighed.

"How do you feel about that?"

"Someone stealing your credit card is something I thought I'd worry about from a stranger, not my wife. She knows my Social Security number and everything else you'd need to open new credit cards. There's no stopping her. I'm married to an identity thief. I just want to be a resident in my own home and not be on constant guard."

"That's really hard, Mitch," the therapist validated.

"So, the question I keep coming back to is how am I supposed to know what's Sonja and what's the disease? It can't just be that all the bad stuff is the disease and all the good stuff is Sonja. I don't have a disease, and I still make bad decisions. Where is the accountability? Where's the line? Where do I insist that she be held responsible, and where do I let it go?"

"Those are all good questions."

"Our whole marriage, I have worked long hours and have paid off her spending. It's exhausting and, quite frankly, unfair. But on the other hand, I don't think she can clean up a mess like this when she's in an episode. We've had dozens of fights about returning what she buys or having her get a job to help pay off her debts, but it creates constant tension in the home. I don't see a middle ground here."

"Perhaps you propose to her that you'll pay off the credit cards she took out in your name but leave her to deal with her own credit card debt," the therapist suggested.

"How on earth would she pay off eighty thousand on her own?" he said, rubbing his temples.

"Let her worry about that. If she doesn't have to deal with consequences, her disease will continue using that method to soothe her. You have to put her outside of her comfort zone to see what she is capable of. Let her feel ownership over some of the debt."

Surprisingly, he felt anxious *for her* at the thought of leaving her to handle a big chunk of debt on her own.

Sonja had gotten released from the psychiatric hospital and was back to taking a drug called Geodon. Mitch came home prepared to play the "therapist-said-so" card to begin holding Sonja accountable.

"Sonja, for the first time in your life, you have to take responsibility of your debt," he said resolutely.

"But how would I pay it off? I have no job, no money," she said, uninterested.

"We've talked about this enough for you to know my answer to that: return the jewelry," he snapped.

"You know I can't do that." Sonja teared up.

For him, it was an obvious fix: return the jewelry and pay off the credit cards. But her obsession with each item ran deep.

"I've enabled you. I shouldn't have paid off your spending for so many years. I can't have you bankrupt the family because you want to buy jewelry," he said quietly.

This type of chaos was giving Mitch his own personal trauma. Even though Mitch was calm, even-tempered, and had loads of fortitude, he had his limits. Most people only change once they've hit rock bottom, and Mitch worried he would hit rock bottom before Sonja did.

CHAPTER 34

A Helping Hand

Mitch sat in the church's beautiful temple full of pristine white furniture, carpets, and a crystal chandelier sparkling in the quiet room and tried to offer some fragments of a prayer to God. But he couldn't focus or find peace like he had with previous prayers. Mitch believed that on some level, God had a plan for him and his family, yet he was starting to question the chaos in his life's journey in that supposed plan. Mitch felt himself fading.

"How is Brother Wasden?"

Mitch looked up and saw a leader of his church congregation standing in front of him, smiling. Mitch didn't know him well, except that he remembered he was a family studies professor and had a tendency to talk slowly and thoughtfully.

"Doing well, Brother Marks," he lied, smiling back.

The man looked down at the floor and seemed to hesitate. "As I looked over at you, it seemed like you had the weight of the world on your shoulders. Is everything okay?"

Mitch was surprised that he had noticed and was ready to brush off his concern again, until he felt something inside crack. Stoically enduring with a stiff upper lip wasn't working for him anymore, and for the first time, Mitch felt the need to share with someone other than a doctor or therapist what his family was going through.

"Actually, things aren't fine," he admitted.

The man sat down next to Mitch and placed his hand on Mitch's shoulder.

"To be honest, they haven't been fine for a long time." He exhaled.

Mitch shared the struggles he was having with Sonja's mental illness and her recent hospitalization. The man listened without judgment or giving advice and assured him that he was there to help, even if all he needed was someone to talk to.

Mitch began meeting with him for an hour each Sunday after church, to talk through everything that was troubling him. He didn't remember much of what Brother Marks said, only how he felt. Mitch felt less alone and took comfort in the fact that there were people around him who cared about his family's struggles.

That experience helped Mitch begin to open up and let other members of his family know of the difficulties he and Sonja were facing. He received a phone call from his mother one evening, just to check in on them.

"I want you to know you have a lot of people praying for you. I let Ann and Aarl Hunter know about your situation." Aarl had been close friends with his father since boyhood. Aarl and his wife were on a church mission in Sweden. "Everyone at the temple in Sweden is praying for you and your family," his mom softly said.

Mitch rarely got emotional, but for some reason, it touched him that another group of people would make an effort to pray on his family's behalf, halfway around the world. He was reminded again that he was not alone but was connected to and supported by more people than he had thought.

Each of these small acts of service did something vital for him. They reaffirmed his faith that there were good people in the world who wanted to help for no other reason than to be kind.

CHAPTER 35

Lincoln Has Enough

December 2015

Sonja frantically called Mitch. "Lincoln ran away!"

"Where'd he go?" he asked, immediately contemplating of all the places his sixteen-year-old son would go.

"I don't know; he just ran outside and kept running till I couldn't keep up." She was panicking.

"But it's snowing!" Mitch said, alarmed.

Mitch snatched his keys off his desk and immediately left work. He drove through the snow, as his windshield wipers struggled against the downpour of sleet. He called Lincoln's friends on his drive home, asking them if they knew where he'd gone. Nothing. He walked through the front door, and Sonja ran into his arms.

"No one's seen him. It's been hours." Sonja hugged him.

"We'll find him," he assured her.

Mitch knew Lincoln had been under immense stress lately. Alex and Rachael were away on church missions, so that left only Lincoln at home. Sonja had manically micromanaged every minute of his day—his friends, homework, tennis, and ACT prep—to the point that he had no time for himself. Mitch started to see exhaustion and frustration in Lincoln's eyes that mirrored his own.

"This schedule you have him on can't continue; you have to see that!" Mitch said, frustrated and panicked.

"This isn't about the schedule. He just had a bad day," she insisted.

Sonja's illness blinded her to the toll this was having on Lincoln. Her OCD and bipolar disorder were a wicked combination. The OCD had an enormous need to control things in minute detail, and the bipolar disorder gave her the energy and drive to execute that controlling tendency to a superhuman degree. But Lincoln wasn't superhuman.

"A bow that is constantly strung will lose its spring," Mitch told her. "Give Lincoln the space to be a kid." He looked at her earnestly.

No matter how many times he told Sonja to ease up on Lincoln, she kept pressing. Mitch drove around the neighborhood and nearby parks, but to no avail.

As he drove into the garage, he wondered if he should call the police. He went inside the house and heard the front door open. Lincoln walked in with snow in his hair.

"Lincoln's home!" Mitch yelled to Sonja in the next room as he wrapped Lincoln in a blanket.

Sonja came running and threw her arms around him. "We love you, Lincoln."

But Lincoln brushed her off.

Mitch walked Lincoln into the living room and turned on the gas fireplace. Lincoln lay down on his side in front of it, silent. Mitch lay down on the floor right next to him with his arm around him.

"I'm sorry, Lincoln. Help me understand what you're feeling," he said.

Lincoln stared at the fire for what felt like an eternity. In the end, he said nothing.

CHAPTER 36

Snapped

December 13, 2015

Several nights later, Lincoln and Sonja were fighting about his schedule once again, and it instantly escalated into a battle of wills.

"Lincoln, I've had enough! Just do your homework!" Sonja screamed.

"I can do it later. I want to go out with my friends." Lincoln opened the fridge.

"Follow the schedule, Lincoln!" Sonja insisted.

"I'm sixteen years old. I can plan my own schedule!" He brushed past her.

"No, you can't!" she screamed back, eyes blazing.

"Guys, knock it off!" Mitch got between them. "There's no need to keep screaming at each other. This is not a hard problem to solve. Sonja, let Lincoln write out his own schedule," Mitch demanded.

"Absolutely not!" Sonja slapped her hands on the kitchen counter.

People say in a marriage you shouldn't disagree in front of your kids or else you won't look unified, but that wasn't an option in their marriage.

"Sonja! Seriously, you have got to stop this! This is insane," Mitch pleaded.

"I think I should write my own schedule!" Lincoln yelled back.

"*No!*" Sonja screamed.

Mitch knew she couldn't fathom giving up that much control, but he had to help his son.

"Sonja, you're done overseeing it! He's writing his own schedule!" Mitch screamed, ending the fight.

"This is all your fault!" Sonja screamed at Lincoln and then ran out of the room.

"She'll be fine," Mitch assured Lincoln. "Just let her blow off some steam."

After heating up some soup, Mitch went to go check on Sonja. She was not in the bedroom, and when he tried to open the master bathroom door, it was locked.

"Sonja, open the door," he demanded. She ignored him. Mitch shook the doorknob, starting to get worried about why she was so silent.

"Sonja, open the door!" he screamed.

Mitch quickly got a paper clip and frantically tried to pick the lock. The lock finally clicked, and he pushed the door open. Sonja was slumped on the bathroom tile with empty pill bottles at her side.

"Sonja!" He ran to her. Mitch held her head in his lap as he frantically dialed 911.

CHAPTER 37

The Next Morning

Feeling like he had just slept off a bad dream, Mitch rolled over to the sound of his alarm that morning and reached his hand out for Sonja. His hand landed in empty sheets. He sat up, getting a clear look at her nightstand scattered with self-help books. Despite her endless attempts to help herself, she now lay in the ICU, with doctors fighting to save her life.

The house was so quiet, yet her fingerprints were everywhere. Her toothbrush, her reading glasses, her chocolate cupboard left open: every object that belonged to Sonja felt sacred all of a sudden. The morning felt strange without her big personality joining Lincoln and him in the kitchen. Mitch glanced at her black velvet heels, which had been tipped on their side by the front door. Imprints of her existed throughout the house, and he worried she'd never come back to give them life.

At work, Mitch's boss, the vice chancellor of health affairs, and the chief medical officer were the only two people who asked how Mitch was doing, while the rest of the people at work chose not to acknowledge that his wife was lying in the ICU five floors above them. It seemed that because it wasn't some physical ailment people could understand that had put her in the ICU, it instantly became delicate ground that no one would tread.

Even though the hospital had put a fake name on his wife's hospital wristband, he felt the whispers, and many people stopped looking him in the eyes when he walked the hospital hallways. Some even outright avoided him. Suicide is a difficult topic for many. It was clear that his presence made those people uncomfortable, and although they were good people, they added to how alone he felt.

Throughout the day, he would take a service elevator to the fifth floor and slip into the ICU to check on Sonja. There was not much to do but sit and watch the monitors and breathing tubes keeping her alive. The doctors let him know that at this point all they could tell him was that she was alive. Mitch needed her to wake up. And if she did, what would he say? Where did they go from here? This was uncharted territory. If she lived, would she attempt suicide again? Would she die from suicide? Her father did.

With suicide, there's a level of uncertainty that forces you to always be on guard, even though you have very little control over the other person. When Sonja was depressed, he took all the medicine in the house with him to work. Advil, cough syrup, everything. Opening cupboards and searching through the house to make sure he hadn't forgotten about pill bottles left in a junk drawer felt just as routine as taking a dog for a walk before work. This was their normal.

Obviously, packing all the medicine in his briefcase couldn't stop her from going to the store and buying new medicine to overdose on. But the activation energy it'd take to go to the store dropped the chances of it happening. *When you're depressed in bed, you don't have the energy to get the keys, drive to Walmart, and buy something*, he would reason in his head. So simply removing an easy temptation lowered the risk.

People could look at Mitch and say, "Your wife is suicidal; you need to watch her more carefully!" But what about when your wife's almost *always* suicidal; should he stay home and watch her forever? When people came to help for a day, they would come in and think they were giving groundbreaking advice, based on the things they observed. "You should stay home from work today; she's clearly at risk." But the reality was she was always at risk. This wasn't a temporary situation. He would never have held down a job if he stayed home every time she was having a bad day.

Mitch looked around at all his friends, and suicide wasn't a part of their marriages. But it played a large role in his, and he knew as long as he stayed married to Sonja, it always would. Sonja had threatened suicide thousands of times, and hundreds of times it was so severe that Mitch took extra precautions. When you avoid failure that many times, you can believe you're good at handling a situation, and that complacency can be dangerous. She had found her medication in his briefcase, which he obviously had not hidden well enough, and now he felt partly responsible.

―✝ ✝―

That night, Lincoln quietly did his homework while he and Mitch sat in Sonja's hospital room. Mitch was lost in his thoughts. He had been watching his sixteen-year-old son slowly fall apart for the last year under the relentlessly controlling environment Sonja's illness created. He knew he couldn't manage the two of them under the same roof, and the doctors said that if Sonja came out of this alive, she would be in no position to be a mother.

What was his responsibility in all this? What did God think and expect of him? Mitch had fought through thousands of battles by Sonja's side, and he knew he loved her with everything he had, but it never seemed to be enough. He was getting destroyed. Where did self-preservation fit in all this? And most importantly, what about Lincoln? What about his role as a father, a protector? He had failed Lincoln, and the one thing he knew with certainty was that Lincoln had to come first, and Sonja and Lincoln couldn't live under the same roof.

Mitch turned to Lincoln. "Do you want to get an apartment with me and have Mom live in our house? We can hire someone to watch her."

"Is she going to live?" Lincoln asked again, his eyes staying focused on his homework sheet. He still avoided looking at his mother lying in the hospital bed.

"I'm not 100 percent sure, but I believe she will," Mitch said, trying to stay positive but honest.

"Do you remember last year when I said I felt I should be living in Utah?" Lincoln looked across Sonja at Mitch.

"Yeah, I remember." Mitch nodded.

"Aunt Leslie said I could live with them in Midway and do high school there. I think I want to do that," Lincoln said.

Mitch didn't know what to say. Out of all the options he had played out in his head, none of them involved losing Lincoln. If he let him go, he wouldn't be there to watch his tennis matches or take pictures at his high school dances or have their late-night talks before bed. Mitch felt like he would be sending him away without protection, but he hadn't been able to protect him in their own home. Guilt overwhelmed him.

"It feels right for me to go to Utah, doesn't it?" Lincoln broke the silence.

Mitch touched Sonja's lifeless hand and then looked at Lincoln. He was losing his family.

"It does." He barely got the words out.

CHAPTER 38

The Bedside Talk

It was lunchtime, and Mitch sat by Sonja's hospital bed, needing to talk to her about their son, even if she was unconscious. He took her hand and put it in his and started the hard conversation.

"I don't know how to tell you this, but Lincoln's moving out. I called Leslie. Lincoln is going to finish high school in Utah and live with them," he told her. The only response he got was the beeps from the heart monitor. "He will start school in Utah after Christmas break." She was lying there so quietly. It was so not her.

Sonja had always been a stop-and-go type of person. When she cooked, it was always on high—it didn't matter what she was cooking. When she drove her car, she would drive until the last drop of gas and barely make it to the gas station. She would talk on her cell phone until the moment it died, and she'd keep shopping until the last item was scanned. She frequently would leave Mitch with the cashier to "quickly" go grab another item while they rang them up. It always panicked him that she wouldn't get back in time, but like clockwork she'd come running with her arms full of more items to add to the pile. She lived on the edge in every category of her life and pushed everything to its limit, including herself.

She pushed harder, faster, and longer than anyone he knew. And when she hit a wall, she would break the wall down instead of acknowledging it was breaking her. It didn't matter how exhausted she was; she worked things into fruition. And that's how she raised their children. Sonja consistently pushed them past their limits and then some. They would often call Mitch in tears, saying they couldn't do what she was asking of them. But time after time, they moved through the unbearable task and achieved exactly what they had set out to achieve. Sonja taught them how to move past failure and grow in a way most people couldn't dream of. But with Lincoln, it was different. Her illness had taken things to a new level, and he saw his child actually starting to crack.

"Lincoln can't live under the same roof as you," he let her know.

He touched her hair and whispered, "And I'm not sure I can either."

His emotions felt like they were all over the place, and he couldn't pin them down. He loved her, and he had fought for their marriage. Yet her mental illness felt like a wrecking ball, demolishing whatever it touched. This suicide attempt and losing Lincoln had obliterated him. He had withstood twenty-three years of mental illness, and he had no more fight left in him.

Mitch took a deep breath. "Sonja, I don't think I can do this anymore." He put her hand back on the hospital bed and left.

CHAPTER 39

Awake

Once Sonja had finally woken up, the doctors and Mitch gathered in her hospital room.

"Mitch, you're here." She struggled to speak louder than a whisper. "How bad was the car accident?"

What? Could she really not remember her suicide attempt? Was she blocking it out?

She continued to look at him. "Am I paralyzed?"

"You're not paralyzed" was the question he chose to answer.

One of the doctors stepped toward her bed. "Sonja, you tried to kill yourself. We think you took over two hundred pills. You're lucky to be alive."

Panicked, she looked at Mitch for assurance, but he gave none.

Another doctor then spoke. "You're in no condition to be a mother right now."

Mitch knew motherhood was everything to Sonja, so he tried to soften the doctor's direct approach. "Sonja, Lincoln is moving to Utah and is going to finish high school there. I gave him the option of living with me in an apartment here in Columbia, but he chose to live with Chris and Leslie in Utah. I think being around his cousins and grandparents might be best for him right now."

She must have sensed just how serious he was; her eyes flashed down to her lap, and she sat quietly.

"We will be back to check on you tomorrow," a doctor said and headed for the door as the others followed him out.

Mitch pulled a chair up by her bed; he had a hard time looking at her.

"I love you," she said, breaking the silence.

He sighed. "I love you too, Sonja. I just can't do what we've been doing anymore." He looked at the tubes in her arms. "All this ... I sat in this room with our son while you were unconscious. Lincoln asked me if his mother would live, and I had to tell him the truth—I didn't know."

"Mitch, I'm so sorry." She choked up.

"For years you have leaned on me. I'm so low right now that I'm even uninterested in living life. I've just been trying to survive and keep our family from coming apart. But now that's happened." He shifted in his seat and took a breath. "I'm going to look for an apartment. You can live in the house. It'll be better for you to be around familiar things and not have to move."

"We're separating?"

"Sonja, I love you; how can I not? You're the mother of my children. Even with your illness, you've always put the kids first, and I've admired that about you. But I think it'd be best for our long-term health if you learned to live a more independent life."

"What do you mean by *independent?*" she softly asked.

"Maybe you need to get a job—something that requires you to wake yourself up in the morning or to shower more often. I just can't keep being the only person keeping things sane."

"Are you going to divorce me?" she asked.

"I'm not sure how this will play out. I haven't thought that far ahead," he admitted.

"I'd understand if you do." She swallowed. "And I'll let you go peacefully. I believe God is proud of you. You've stuck with me through thick and thin, and I'm grateful for that. I don't want to cause you any more pain. But I will fight for you, our marriage, and our family. I love you. You're my soul mate. I will do whatever

I have to do to keep you." She reached her hand as far out as she could to his, but he did not move to bridge the gap.

He struggled to be hopeful that things could be fixed. Her admissions were sincere in that moment, but history had taught him that their life always seemed to regress to a predictable chaos that he could no longer live with. He didn't doubt her love, or his for her, but it appeared in this case that love would not conquer all.

His phone started ringing. "Yeah, Linc? All right. I'll be home soon." He put his phone in his pocket and looked at her briefly. "I have to go."

Their family bond at times felt as fragile as a worn piece of thread that had somehow held up, but now it had snapped. He was drowning, and there was no one to save him but him.

Sonja had been in the hospital for over a week and was finally released. Her best friend, Lorie, had taken her home. Mitch drove home that night from work, unsure what he would be dealing with when he got there.

"Hi, Mitch!" Sonja happily greeted him. "Are you hungry? Should I make some dinner for you?" she eagerly asked.

"No, that's okay. I'm just going to go to bed," he said a bit distantly. He appreciated that she was trying but didn't want to give her false hope.

"Well, how was your day?" she asked, following him into their bedroom. He stopped her in the doorway.

"I think it would be best if we slept in separate rooms." He steadily looked her in the eyes.

After all the arguments and crazy things she had done, he had always allowed them to go back to the way they were once it was over. But this time was different. He desperately needed space.

Later that night, he went to lock the doors and heard Sonja's oxygen machine in her bedroom. The hospital required her to sleep with oxygen because at night she would suddenly stop breathing. The doctors were not sure why but concluded it had something to do with the overdose. The soft sound of her oxygen tank was a loud reminder of what had happened.

Sonja and Mitch had become accustomed to their difficulties. He hadn't seen the damage caused amid the flames and smoke, but as things settled down, it became clear. Mitch was looking through settled ash and quiet embers, and for once he saw *each* of their scalded souls.

His wife's.

His son's.

His own.

And Mitch wasn't sure he could risk living in a fire hazard again.

CHAPTER 40

The Holidays

Mitch sat on the airplane with Lincoln and a quiet Sonja. They were on their way to Utah to drop Lincoln off at his brother's house to start a new, bipolar-free life. They would be also celebrating Christmas at his parents' house. Mitch had brought several apartment brochures he intended to review so he could make a final decision about his future living arrangements.

Throughout the years, Mitch had asked himself, *Why am I pushing through this?* One reason had been because he loved Sonja. He thought when they got older and life was less stressful, their relationship would get better. Another huge motive for pushing through in the past was that he wanted to keep their family intact. But now his family had blown up, and that reason had disappeared. She had hurt him in a way that wasn't mending. In a way that erased hope for a better future together.

Rachael wouldn't be home for another four months and Alex in eleven months from their church missions. So, they decided not to tell them about Sonja's suicide attempt and their new family situation until they could do so face-to-face. Mitch and Sonja did not want to disturb their mission experience and have them worry about what was going on at home.

"How are you feeling?" he asked Lincoln.

"Good. I think not living at home will be better for me." Lincoln sighed. "But Dad"—he paused—"you're still living with Mom." He looked at him, worried. Lincoln knew he needed to get out but was concerned that Mitch had to stay.

"It'll be okay, Linc."

Mitch hadn't told Lincoln that he was separating from Sonja and that there was a real possibility they would end up divorced. He felt Lincoln already had too much to deal with and didn't need his parents' marriage added to the pile.

Mitch had told Sonja's sisters and brothers that he was moving out. He wanted them to be able to support her. He shared some information with his parents and siblings about Sonja and his situation but not anything about the state of their marriage. He was sitting on that information because he didn't feel centered enough to share anything with his own family. Over the years, he often chose to keep their marriage difficulties to himself, so as not to burden family members with problems they couldn't solve.

Mitch was guarded in what he spoke about. He and Sonja slept in different bedrooms at his parents' house, which he knew they couldn't fail to notice, but his parents didn't say anything. His parents always respected their children's privacy.

That night, everyone sat around the kitchen table eating sugar cookies Mitch's mother had made.

"So, Mom and I are going to do some Christmas shopping tonight. Is there anything we should remember?" Mitch cheerfully asked Lincoln. With everything that had gone on, they hadn't gotten around to Christmas shopping.

"I don't know." Lincoln shrugged. "Anything's good." He seemed distant, and Mitch noticed Lincoln still refused to look at Sonja. He worried that no amount of time would soften these wounds.

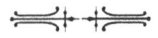

Like the functional, happy parents they were not, Sonja and Mitch left the house and drove to the mall.

"What do you think we should get him?" Sonja asked.

"There are a few places I want to stop in the mall. I think they'll have something he'll like," Mitch quickly responded.

He readjusted his hands on the steering wheel as he drove through the snow, with Christmas carols playing on the radio. Wreaths hung on streetlamps, and trees were pinned with colorful lights, but it all felt wasted on him. Holidays are usually a time when people come together and ground themselves in their family ties. But that Christmas emphasized all the ways his family was breaking.

"Wow, look at the tree." Sonja pointed.

He looked over at her smiling face but found it hard to reciprocate. Her very presence radiated every painful event that had led up to his breaking point. He hated that he felt that way. He hated that he couldn't smile at her like she was at him. She looked too innocent to be held accountable for the crimes that had contributed to his hurt, yet that didn't stop the hurt from swallowing every other emotion. They walked into the crowded mall and kicked snow off their shoes on the large mats at the entrance.

"Should we stop at Build-A-Bear? I know he's sixteen, but he still loves those things," she happily suggested.

He could sense her eagerness to get along and patch things up, and it made him uncomfortable. He planned on moving out, and she needed to accept that was happening.

"I just ... I need space away from you," he said apologetically.

She instantly got quiet.

"I'm not trying to be mean."

"Okay." She swallowed. "Just call me then when you're ready to leave."

The mall played Christmas songs throughout the stores, and a larger-than-life tree shimmered at the entrance. The shoppers holding hands and the bouncy tunes taunted him. He wanted to celebrate; he wanted to feel the magic that every other Christmas had brought his family. But this year he was an observer, a window-shopper to everyone else's holiday spirit.

CHAPTER 41

Losing Lincoln

"You got everything?" Sonja asked Lincoln.

"Yeah," he answered, sitting on the bed looking at Mitch. They heard Mitch's brother Chris and his wife, Leslie, talking upstairs. They had come to pick up Lincoln.

The reality hit him hard that he was leaving behind his teenage son, who was soon to be hundreds of miles away. Tears threatened to push their way out. Mitch swallowed them back, wanting to be strong for Lincoln. He grabbed some of Lincoln's luggage and followed him up to the main floor.

"Lincoln, you ready to go?" Leslie cheerfully said, hugging him.

Mitch's stomach clenched, and instantly he felt sick. Everything that was happening made him feel like he couldn't breathe.

"I love you, Lincoln." He couldn't hold back the tears as he hugged his son goodbye. Mitch couldn't let him go, and they stood there tightly hugging each other as they both cried.

He felt anger toward Sonja. She had made a choice that now affected his ability to be a father and Lincoln's ability to be a kid. She had jeopardized his son's well-being, and he had not been able to stop it in time. The weight of that guilt lay heavily on him. This event would leave a lifelong wound on Lincoln that only God and therapy could heal, but he knew it would still leave a nasty scar.

Mitch and Sonja watched Lincoln get into the car with Leslie to start an entirely new life. His brother stopped in the doorway, and Mitch grabbed him in a hug.

"Thank you, brother," Mitch cried. His brother held him tight.

His brother was doing something for Mitch that he could not do himself—parent his child. Mitch knew Chris and Leslie would treat Lincoln like their own, and that brought him some comfort.

Sonja and Mitch flew home in silence—something about suffering makes silence loud. He was so caught up in his own emotions that he didn't even register what Sonja was doing when they were saying goodbye to Lincoln. He just needed space away; he needed to clear his head. Mitch felt his identity as a father being lost. His sense of self had vanished into this being who was simply enduring life. When he looked in the mirror, he didn't recognize himself anymore. He needed a moment to himself. A long moment.

When they got home to an empty house, Lincoln's absence stung deeper. Mitch went into their bedroom alone, shutting the door behind him, still not saying a single word to Sonja. He felt there was nothing left to say. Lincoln was gone.

CHAPTER 42

Appearances

Sonja and Mitch stepped into a glittering ballroom, for a fundraising gala raising money for heart disease that his hospital was sponsoring, without so much as brushing arms. It felt important to put on a brave face and get the public awkwardness of what had happened behind them. She looked every bit the part in diamonds and a black velvet dress as they were greeted by the chancellor, deans of each college, and the president of the university. On the outside, they looked like a perfectly dressed, happy couple, yet they were severely bruised and broken on the inside.

Sonja had nerves of steel as she mingled for hours in a room full of people aware she had attempted suicide. He watched her as she shook hands with each one of them with a grace that seemed akin to that of nobility.

Every person smiled at her and acted like nothing had happened. If she had been in a car wreck and had almost died, Mitch knew every person would stop to ask her how she was doing. He knew it was painful for her to be there for that reason and because they were separating. But Sonja was Sonja, and she would support him to the end.

"Are you ready to go?" he asked. "It's getting late." These were the first words he had spoken to her all night.

"Yes." She looked wearily at him. They walked to the car in

silence, with her high heels clicking on the cement being the only sound between them.

He turned to her once they were home. "Thank you for coming," he said politely.

"You're welcome." She stood looking at him.

Mitch walked away to the bedroom where he was sleeping, and Sonja walked in the opposite direction to hers.

CHAPTER 43

The Unexpected

Mitch looked in the dining room and saw the table covered with jewelry. Trays of rings and bracelets glistened in stacks, as Sonja busily typed on her computer.

"What are you doing?" His pulse started to race. She had eBay pulled up on her computer, and anxiety immediately sparked through him.

"I'm selling my jewelry. Lorie and I have been working on it all week." She kept typing.

"What?" he said in disbelief, barely able to get the word out.

He knew when a piece of jewelry sneaked away from her, it only increased her obsessive nature to have it. But now, without a word, Sonja was uploading photos of her collection on eBay.

"But what about your OCD?" He looked at all the jewelry on the table.

"Dialectical behavior therapy is teaching me how to get comfortable with being uncomfortable." She mournfully looked at her jewelry.

Dialectical behavior therapy (DBT) was a therapy they had been unaware existed. They had done all sorts of therapy, including counseling, psychotherapy, exposure, behavioral activation, cognitive behavioral, and EMDR.

After Sonja had attempted suicide, Lorie spent days on her computer researching more therapies and talking to therapists.

She discovered DBT, a scientifically based therapy, and helped Sonja get into the yearlong program. DBT teaches skills. The first is mindfulness, the ability to radically accept things as they are and be present in the moment. The second is distress tolerance, which is the ability to tolerate negative emotions instead of trying to escape from them. The third is emotional regulation, which teaches you the ability to manage and change intense and problematic emotions. The fourth is interpersonal effectiveness, which teaches you to communicate with others in a way that is assertive, maintains self-respect, and strengthens relationships.

"And you feel like it's working?" he asked, a bit skeptical.

"Yes."

"I see." He eyed her.

Her obsession with jewelry ran deep, and yet here she sat, ready to get rid of pieces. A conversation around selling her jewelry no longer caused her to thrash around like a trapped animal; she was openly sad about it, but willing.

"Either way, I need to pay off my debt," she said.

This was the first time in their marriage that she was actually taking responsibility for the damage her illness had inflicted on their family.

He didn't know what to say to her newfound clarity. Then he suddenly noticed her outfit. "Why are you all dressed up?" he asked.

"I got a job," she casually said.

"What?" He stood, not moving.

"I'm working retail at White House Black Market in the mall," she informed him.

Sonja hadn't worked outside the home for over twenty years. He had serious doubts that she could maintain a job and work with customers, given how many bad days she had. While he knew a minimum-wage job would never come close to paying off her debt, he was impressed that she was making an attempt.

"Wow. Congratulations," he said, still not moving.

"Thank you." She smiled broadly. "Mitch, I'm not only fighting for a good life." She looked up at him. "I'm fighting for you."

CHAPTER 44

Heartache

Mitch continued to research apartments online and take tours of the ones he was interested in. It had been months, and he was still living with Sonja, even though they were in separate bedrooms. He wanted something close to work that allowed pets, in case he ever ended up getting a dog to keep him company, but none of the current apartment complexes felt right.

"I'll be on a walk." Sonja rushed through the room, putting on a big hat, even though her face was already pasted white in SPF 100 plus sunscreen mixed with zinc. Mitch watched her through the dining room window as she put in her earphones and pumped her arms. She was totally unaware that her thick sweater was inside out, as were her leggings, as she danced through the cold streets.

There was a method to mindfulness that suggested when the present moment is hard to feel, you should shake up your routine to "wake up" to what is happening right then. Some people did subtle things, like running their hands on walls as they walked or looking up at the sky and then their feet. Sonja's favorite method of grounding was dancing each morning through the neighborhood.

He watched as she wholeheartedly embraced mindfulness and practiced every skill she got her hands on. DBT had introduced mindfulness in a way Sonja could not only understand it but also practice it. She was working very hard on letting go of the past and not worrying about the future. Sonja was striving to live in the moment. Her methods were charming, and her persistence was notable.

The questions he asked himself as he watched her embrace the now were *Could I let go of our past? Could I not worry about the future and live in each moment with Sonja?* She was ready to move on and build a better life for herself. She was actively trying to repair the hurt between them, but he was stuck. Something kept him from openly pushing through and loving her again.

As he watched her throw her arms up and tilt her massive hat up to the sky to take in the sunrise, he realized she wasn't scared. She was confronting her demons and seemed to finally feel like she had the armor and bravery to win against them.

His fears focused on not letting her fully back into his life. Her suicide attempt had hurt him in ways he could never put into words, and he never wanted to give one person enough of him to cut that deep again.

Mitch pulled into the driveway after work and saw Sonja dressed in all black, lovingly pruning her rosebushes. Her cheek leaned into her phone screen as she talked on the phone. She looked so focused—her brow furrowed and neck positioned deep inside the thorny bushes. She loved her roses, and as he watched her, he began to feel endeared to her again. Not romantically, as a husband looking at his wife, but as a person seeing the sensitivity inside another.

He got out of the car with his briefcase, and she looked up and gave him a huge smile and wave. He waved back and walked into the house. He took his dinner into their bedroom and turned on his favorite TV series, *Modern Family*.

Splash!

He heard the sound of water slapping around in the kitchen and ran out to see what had happened. All he saw was Sonja throwing her entire face into a large bowl of ice water.

"What are you doing?" He watched the water spill over the edges of the bowl.

She pulled her dripping face from the bowl and took a sharp breath.

"TIPS," she said quickly between breaths. "It's a DBT skill for anxiety," she said before sinking her face back in the icy water.

"Does it work?" he asked, watching her face sit beneath the water and ice cubes. This seemed like a strange way to go about treating anxiety, but he was intrigued.

Her wet face once again emerged from the ice.

"The shock of the ice water kind of resets my brain when I'm in trouble. I'm learning skills, Mitch. For the first time, I'm not fighting this illness or pleading with God to take it away. I'm learning to live *with* it." She dried her face off with a kitchen towel. "Cool, huh?" She smiled proudly.

He just stood staring at her, not sure what to say.

She emptied out the ice water in the sink and walked over to the pantry.

"Alexa, play 'Don't Stop Believing' by Journey," she yelled, getting herself a piece of chocolate and turning back to him. "Having an illness doesn't mean I can't enjoy life." Sonja closed her eyes, enjoying the chocolate. *"Just a small-town girl ..."* The music pounded through the speakers.

Sonja danced to the music and sang along as she began unloading the dishwasher. Sonja and Mitch had so much history together that despite his current hesitancy, it felt natural to slide back into old patterns. He picked up a broom and started to help clean the kitchen by sweeping the floor. He then began to hum to the song.

Sonja stood in front of him, looking into his eyes, and he stared right back into hers, seeing the girl from the mansion who opened the door all those years ago. She kissed him, and memories of their first kiss on that BYU dance floor came flooding back, along with the countless kisses over the years. Then the memory of him kissing her lifeless body on the bathroom floor immediately had his mind screaming, *No!* And just as quickly as the kissing had begun, it ended as he stepped away.

"No, Sonja. Just no." He shook his head.

Mitch walked back into their bedroom with his half-eaten dinner and shut the door behind him. There was instant pain, and he closed his eyes. His heart ached. It ached for her. But it also ached because of her.

CHAPTER 45

Relationships

Mitch walked in from work to find Sonja crying on the couch. *And we're back to normal,* he thought.

She sat against decorative pillows, wiping away tears as she wrote in her DBT workbook. He sat next to her, prepared for anything. She looked up from her book.

"You need something?" she asked, blowing her nose.

"Um, no. Do you need something?" he asked, confused.

"Nope." She shook her head.

"But you're crying," he pointed out.

"Obviously." She rolled her eyes. "Mitch, I lost the privilege of raising our sixteen-year-old son. All I've ever known is being a mother." She placed her hand on her heart. "Even though we visit him every month in Utah, I have a lot of work to do to repair that relationship. My therapist said it's okay to cry, but I have to do my DBT homework to learn how to have better relationships. So, I'm kinda busy right now. Can we talk later?" She squinted her eyes apologetically.

"Uh, yeah." He got up, stunned. *She doesn't need me to comfort her? And she's working on her own, without my help?* he thought.

At that moment, it hit him like a bolt of lightning that she was going to be fine with or without him. But wait! Did he want her to be okay without him?

CHAPTER 46

Fighting for Love

Like a moth to the flame, Sonja stopped at the flower department as they did the grocery shopping for the week. She got a light in her eyes while looking at each vase.

"Do you want to get some flowers?" Mitch asked.

"You wouldn't mind?" She bit her lip.

"Not at all," he said.

"Thank you," she said, carefully deciding which one to bring home. She settled on some baby pink roses. An unconscious smile spread across her face, the same one she would get during romantic scenes in a movie.

"I'm not exactly buying you flowers," he said for clarification. Mitch hoped she was not taking this as a romantic gesture. "It's part of our grocery budget, so you can spend it on things you like too."

"I know." She smiled. "I still love them."

They brought them home, and she placed them as a table centerpiece, still beaming.

"Well, I've got some work I need to do," he said, gesturing toward the bedroom.

"Okay. And Mitch—"

"Yeah?"

"Thanks again for the flowers," she said as he closed the door.

Mitch sat on his bed, going through new apartment brochures

he had gotten that day. He still hadn't moved out. He didn't know why he hadn't pulled the trigger. He just kept looking at apartment after apartment without signing any paperwork. Something was holding him back.

Sonja knocked on the bedroom door and walked in.

"Mitch, I need to talk to you."

"About what?" he asked, worried it was about his decision to leave or why he hadn't left yet, because he still didn't know why either.

"Dialectical behavior therapy is changing my life. I need to apologize to you." She looked straight into his eyes. "I'm taking ownership of this illness, which I've never done in the past. I've forced you to carry too much of it and then blamed you when I didn't feel it go away. I lashed out instead of accepting responsibility." She took a big breath. "This illness is mine to take care of and manage. It's not my mom's, sisters', brothers', children's, or your responsibility. People can support me, and that is enough."

Mitch felt his chest get physically lighter. Finally, there was room to breathe because there was room between her illness and him.

She continued, "I didn't do anything to deserve this illness, but nevertheless"—she threw a finger in the air—"it's mine to take care of! My happiness and well-being are no one's responsibility but mine."

He'd never heard Sonja talk about her illness this way before. The DBT program was the first time he saw therapy making real improvements. She seemed different. There was a clarity in her eyes that he hadn't seen in years.

"I've been so angry that I have an illness that I failed to see there are thousands of people with crippling illnesses doing life; I'm not the only one." She grabbed his hand, and he let her. "I want to fight for this marriage. We have had children together, done careers; you have been to hell and back with me, and I want to come out the other end better for it."

"I'm not—" He took his hand back.

"Let me finish." She stopped him. "I need you to know that you can walk away from this, from me. You can leave this illness and never deal with it again." She looked at him seriously. "I will let you go because I love you, and I will be okay."

At that moment, he realized he truly could walk away from mental illness and suicide. Sonja couldn't make that choice. She could never walk away from those struggles. But he could. He could walk free.

"But until you serve me divorce papers, I will fight for you!" She left with those words hanging in the air.

Later that week, Sonja came through the back door with Old Navy shopping bags. She pulled a pair of navy-blue jeans out of the plastic bag and handed them to Mitch. "I want you to try these on. After work, I stopped to pick you up some jeans."

"Oh, thanks." He stood stunned.

She never bought him things unless it was his birthday or Christmas. This was so out of the ordinary; he wasn't sure how to accept the gift.

"Like now?" he asked, taking the jeans from her.

"Yeah, I want to see if they fit." She waved him into the bathroom.

He closed the bathroom door and held the heavy denim in his hands. The idea that Sonja had been at a store and had thought of him and that he needed jeans was unusually meaningful to him. It was evidence that there was a small opening or crack in the wall that had emotionally separated them.

CHAPTER 47

Freedom to Choose

Mitch stared at the apartment lease in front of him. The office manager waited for him to sign as he held the pen in his hand, not moving. For the first time in his life, he felt released, free. He could leave Sonja without any guilt; everyone would understand. He gripped the pen in his sweaty hand and stared blankly at the black printed words they wanted him to agree to.

Then he set the pen to the paper. A strong feeling came over him: *This is wrong!* He took a breath, picking the pen back up, but again he couldn't bring himself to sign.

Mitch reflected on his feelings from over the past few months. He missed her even though he had seen her that same day. Thinking about a life where he wouldn't see her made him miss her even more. He couldn't imagine a life without Sonja's idiosyncrasies interrupting his day.

She'd call five times in under five minutes while he was in a board meeting and would send a string of texts all saying, "CALL ME ASAP."

Even though it happened almost daily, he always wondered if this time something had actually happened to her or the kids, so he'd step out of the meeting and call her back.

"Sonja? What is it?" he'd ask.

"Okay, I'm at Target. What's 40 percent off $29.99?"

He smiled, thinking of her oddities. She was all over the place in day-to-day things but focused and strong in the things that mattered. The memory of her protecting him in graduate school still made him laugh.

During graduate school, one of Mitch's friends had made fun of how poorly Mitch had done on a finance test in front of their classmates. When Sonja found out about the student mocking him, she knocked on his apartment door.

"So, grades determine what type of person you are or how successful you will be?" she fumed. "Making fun of a friend behind their back says more about you than it does about him. Don't you *ever* speak negatively about my husband. He has been a good friend to you. You should be ashamed of the way you behaved, laughing behind his back."

Later, that same friend showed up at their apartment in tears and apologized to Mitch for what he had said. Sonja went to war for the people she loved. And she loved Mitch fiercely.

Even through all the hell she had brought into his life, if he was honest with himself, he was proud to be her husband. What Sonja had and continued to go through should have shattered her to the point that she couldn't go on. Life punched Sonja *hard* to the ground, yet *every* time she would get back up. This crisis had revealed to Mitch what he already knew about Sonja: she embodied courage. These past months he had watched Sonja tirelessly work and struggle to gain the DBT skills to create a life worth living, despite having a mental illness, and she was making real improvements.

Did he want to continue to be a part of Sonja's journey? Unlike the first time around, if he chose her, he would go into the marriage fully knowing what he was getting himself into. He had always told her, "I would pick you again." But now he actually had that choice.

He set down the pen.

"I'm not going to need that apartment after all." Mitch stood up and ran back to the car.

When he walked into the house, he was greeted by Sonja carrying a larger-than-life get-well-soon card.

"Mitch!" Sonja welcomed him.

"Sonja, we need to talk." He stopped her. He needed to clear things up before anything else was said.

"Is it about you moving out?" she asked.

"Yes. I went to sign the lease today—"

"Wait!" she shouted. "Just wait." She nervously breathed. "Please read this before you say anything else." She pushed the giant envelope forward. "Just read it."

He opened the large, floppy card and read it. She had written out all the reasons she loved him and why she was sorry for making him sick too. She had taped a picture of herself laughing from their college days inside. He teared up, not saying anything for a moment as he gathered his voice. He was making the right decision.

"Thank you," he said, choked up.

"Did I change your mind about leaving?" she asked.

"No." He laughed.

"What?"

"Because when I went to sign the lease today, I felt like it was the absolute wrong thing to do. I walked away from it. I'm staying here with you." Sonja jumped into his arms, hugging him tight.

He wasn't staying out of obligation or for the children. There were no reasons left to stay except for the very most important one. He was staying because he wanted to.

"You know, I was prepared to bake your favorite oatmeal-raisin cookies every day to win you back."

"Hmm. Cookies would still be a good idea." He put her down and held up the picture. "I always loved that picture of you."

"I want you to put that picture by your nightstand and remember me that way," she said.

Mitch gathered her back into his arms and kissed her like it was their first kiss on the dance floor all those years ago. Choosing her just felt right; from the moment he met her, it always had.

Sonja was worth standing in the fire for.

EPILOGUE

It's been over five years since my mom's suicide attempt. My parents have a happy, fulfilling marriage, and you don't have to take my word for it. When interviewing my dad before writing this book, I asked him to describe his marriage now. He replied:

"Staying was definitely not the easier road, but for me, it was the right one. I had to let go of the past while at the same time not fearing the future. Is her illness still a part of our life? Yes, it is. I live mindfully with her each day and embrace the present moment, no matter what that moment is. We continually work toward what we value most: *us*. I often wonder who I would be without all the suffering your mom and I endured. I've come to realize I'm a deeper, richer person because of her mental illness. I now have a beautiful and complex, but very possible, marriage."

THE IMPOSSIBLE SERIES:

An Impossible Life: Sonja's Story
An Impossible Wife: Mitch's Story
An Impossible Childhood: Rachael's Story
A Possible Life: Sonja Creates a Life Worth Living

Cover Photo
The cover for *An Impossible Wife* was taken by Rachael in 2016, six months after her mom's suicide attempt.

For family pictures and more information go to www.animpossiblelife.com.

AN IMPOSSIBLE CHILDHOOD

Rachael's Story
Keep Reading for a Sneak Peek!

by
Rachael Siddoway

CHAPTER 1

Dear Santa

From the moment I was swaddled in my mother's arms, life was explained to me with no filters or guardrails. There were no cushions to fall back on or watered-down versions to swallow. My mom always shared the truth as she saw it. The things she was honest about were rarely age-appropriate, but like most kids, I was utterly unaware where my family sat on the spectrum of normalcy until later in life. I was treated as her equal, her best friend, and that meant she shared everything with me—even the realities of Santa.

"I need you to help me write a letter to Santa," I told my mom on the way home from preschool.

"Well, you can't write a letter to Santa." She shook her head, quickly pulling into the McDonald's drive-thru.

"Why not?" I asked.

"Because he's dead." She fished out quarters from the cupholder.

"Santa's dead?" I scrunched my face, leaning back into my car seat.

"He was a real man in history, but he died a long time ago. Dad and I buy your presents." She rolled down her window and yelled, "I'll get a kid's meal and a Big Mac!" My mom then turned her head and looked at me. "I thought you knew that."

"So why does everyone at school still write to him?" I looked at her, confused.

"Because their parents haven't told them the truth." She turned and grabbed the bag of food through the window. And just like that, what took most parents years to build up to happened in two minutes at the drive-thru.

For me, it wasn't earth-shattering or shocking to learn that Santa had died, because my parents never really perpetuated the idea that he was alive. Santa and I didn't have any history together; he was just the man in all my Christmas movies and the largest inflatable lawn decoration at Home Depot. But that was not the case for other kids, and soon, at my preschool Christmas party, that was something I was about to find out.

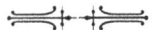

"How does Santa even get down the chimney?" Samantha asked, a mouthful of cookie crumbs dropping on the red plastic tablecloth. "Magic. Same way he makes reindeer fly," Gabby said decidedly.

"But like, how?" Samantha chewed.

I sat and listened to my peers muse over how Santa could eat hundreds of cookies in one night and if his sleigh was really red.

"What do you think, Rachael?" the girl sitting next to me asked.

I took a big bite of my sugar cookie and drank enough milk for the chalky texture to leave the roof of my mouth. "Santa's dead," I proclaimed. All sets of eyes stopped and looked at me.

"No, he's not!" A boy with freckles glared.

I sat up a little straighter. "My *mom* told me he was a real man, but then he died." I knew pulling the Mom card gave me some leverage. They looked at each other in disbelief.

"Santa can't die!" they agreed.

"Besides, who gives the *whole world* presents then?" the freckled boy smugly asked.

One girl rallied the group. "Rachael's a liar!" she shouted.

"I'm not lying." I sank in my chair.

"Rachael hates Santa!" The freckled boy pointed at me.

I was ambushed, and no one believed me. I was a lone soldier in this winter war for truth, and before snack time was over, I had become the most unpopular person at my table. I gripped the sides of my chair as they froze me out and continued their festive conversation.

"What type of cookies should I leave out?" Gabby asked.

"Your mom's favorite cookies," I grumbled.

"Why?" She scrunched her face at me.

"Because she eats the cookies! And she buys the presents!" I yelled in bottled-up frustration.

"Stop lying!" she screamed in my face.

"Girls, girls, what is going on!" The teacher rushed over.

"Rachael said Santa died!" She pointed a stiff finger at me and broke down in tears.

"But it's true!" I looked up at Ms. Allan. *Say I'm right, please say I'm right!* I begged in my mind. The only thing getting me out of peer isolation this Christmas was an adult testimonial, but it was one I would never get.

That winter, I was the outcast. I was left to play by myself at recess, and during reading time, I was pushed out of the reading circle. At an incredibly young age, I was forced to learn how to navigate the volatile seas of not having a typical mother. And most waves were not as inconsequential as burying Santa.

Made in the USA
Monee, IL
04 October 2021